The Cotton Patch Version of Paul's Epistles

The Cotton Patch Version

of Paul's Epistles

CLARENCE JORDAN

Association Press
NEW WIN PUBLISHING, INC.

THE COTTON PATCH VERSION OF PAUL'S EPISTLES

Copyright© 1968 by
Clarence Jordan

This translation by Dr. Jordan is based on the Nestle-Aland Greek text, twenty-third edition (1957).

Printing Code

23 24 25 26 27 28 29 30

International Standard Book Number: 0-8329-1041-4

Library of Congress Catalog Card Number: 82-60871

Printed in the United States of America

Contents

Introduction 7

The Letter to the Christians in Washington *(Romans)* . . . 15

A Letter to the Christians in Atlanta *(I Corinthians)* 47

The Second Letter to the Atlanta Christians *(II Corinthians)* . 75

The Letter to the Churches of the Georgia Convention
(Galatians) 94

The Letter to the Christians in Birmingham *(Ephesians)* . . 105

The Letter to the Alabaster African Church, Smithville,
Alabama *(Philippians)* 115

The Letter to the Christians in Columbus *(Colossians)* . . . 122

The First Letter to the Selma Christians *(I Thessalonians)* . 129

The Second Letter to the Christians in Selma
(II Thessalonians) 135

The First Letter to Timothy 139

The Second Letter to Timothy 147

Titus 153

The Letter to Philemon 157

Introduction

Why a "cotton patch" version? While there have been many excellent translations of the Scriptures into modern English, they still have left us stranded in some faraway land in the long-distant past. We need to have the good news come to us not only in our own tongue but in our own time. We want to be *participants* in the faith, not merely spectators. When Jesus told the story of "a certain man going down from Jerusalem to Jericho," every person in his audience may have felt as though *he* himself were that "certain man" who fell among thieves on the familiar and oft-traveled road. But few of *us* would feel so personally involved. To give us a sense of participation or involvement, that "certain man" would need to be going from New York to Boston, or from Atlanta to Savannah, or from San Francisco to Los Angeles, or from our hometown to the next one. So the "cotton patch" version is an attempt to translate not only the words but the events. We change the setting from first-century Palestine to twentieth-century America. We ask our brethren of long ago to cross the time-space barrier and talk to us not only in modern English but about modern problems, feelings, frustrations, hopes and assurances; to work beside us in our cotton patch or on our assembly line, so that the word becomes modern *flesh.* Then perhaps, we too will be able to joyfully tell of "that which *we* have heard, which *we* have seen with our eyes and have felt with our hands, about the word of life" (I John 1:1).

Another reason for a "cotton patch" version is that the Scriptures should be taken out of the classroom and stained-glass sanctuary and put out under God's skies where people are toiling and crying and wondering, where the mighty events of the good news first happened and where alone they feel at home. We want Paul's letters to have the simplicity, the humbleness, the earthiness which they had before Christians erected temples of mortar and stone.

Still another reason is that the locale of these letters is the South. Cotton has figured prominently in the problems of this region—problems to which the letters eloquently and pointedly and compassionately speak. But by so pinpointing the South, there is no intention of hoarding or limiting God's wisdom to any one section of the world. The gospel is not provincial, even though its birthplace was a remote province of the Roman Empire. People from afar understand this, for the wise men from the distant East are frequently more sensitive to starlight than is the local innkeeper who flashes his "no vacancy" sign.

Perhaps the main reason, though, is that the major portion of my life has been spent on a farm in southwest Georgia where I have struggled for a meaningful expression of my discipleship to Jesus Christ. With my companions along the dusty rows of cotton, corn and peanuts, the Word of Life has often come alive with encouragement, rebuke, correction and insight. I have witnessed the reenactment of one New Testament event after another until I can scarcely distinguish the original from its modern counterpart. And because the present participants are for the most part, like their predecessors, humble people, I have longed to share God's word with them. So in making the translation, I have kept in mind the little people of great faith who want to do better in their discipleship but have been hindered by big words they don't understand or by ancient concepts they don't grasp.

Of course, one can never make a perfect translation even from one contemporary language to another, simply because words seldom have precise equivalents in a different language. It is even more difficult when the two languages are also separated by thousands or even hundreds of years. Then add the barriers of culture and space and the task is indeed formidable. I readily admit, then, that my attempts to find present-day equivalents to many New Testament expressions and concepts are often strained, crude and perhaps even inaccurate. For example, there just isn't any word in our vocabulary which adequately translates the Greek word for "crucifixion." *Our* crosses are so shined, so polished, so respectable that to be impaled on one of them would seem to be a blessed experience. We have thus emptied the term "crucifixion" of its original content of terrific emotion, of violence, of indignity and stigma, of defeat. I have translated it as "lynching," well aware that this is not technically correct. Jesus was officially tried and legally condemned, elements generally lacking in a lynching. But having observed the operation of Southern "justice," and at times having been its victim, I can testify that more people have been lynched "by judicial action" than by unofficial ropes. Pilate at least had the courage and the honesty to publicly wash his hands and disavow all legal responsibility. "See to it yourselves," he told the mob. And they did. They crucified him in Judea and they strung him up in Georgia, with a noose tied to a pine tree.

Likewise, there is no adequate equivalent of "Jew and Gentile." My translation as "white man and Negro" is clear evidence of superimposing my own personal feelings, which is the unpardonable sin of a self-respecting translator. But in the Southern context, is there any other alternative? The same is true with expressions such as "eating meat sacrificed to idols" (I Cor. 8:4), which I translate as "working on Sunday." As strained as this may be, it was just the best I could do. We are faced with the same dilemma in "baptism," "circumcision" and a host of other words too numerous to mention. When I have strayed too far afield, I beg your forgiveness and patience, pleading that you keep in mind my plight.

There are places where it will appear that I have taken entirely too much liberty with the text. But let me point out that this is a translation, not of Paul's *words,* but of his *ideas.* If his actual words convey the wrong impression to a modern hearer, or if they make Paul say something which he obviously did not intend, then I do scuttle his words in favor of his idea. For example, someone would be perfectly understood if he wrote to a friend, "We had hot dogs and Coke for lunch, fish and hush puppies for supper, and then sat around shooting the bull until midnight." But let that letter get lost for about two thousand years, then let some Ph.D. try to translate it into a non-English language of A.D. 3967. If he faithfully translated the *words* it might run something like this: "We had steaming canines (possibly a small variety such as the Chihuahua —*Ed.*) and processed coal (the coke was probably not eaten but used to heat the dogs—*Ed.*) for the noon meal, and fish and mute, immature dogs (no doubt the defective offspring of the hot dog, with which twentieth-century Americans were so preoccupied—*Ed.*) for the evening meal, followed by passively engaging until midnight in the brutish sport of bull-shooting (the bulls were then processed into a large sausage called *bologna*, which sounded like "baloney"—*Ed.*)." For such exacting scholarship the good doctor may have won world renown as the foremost authority on twentieth-century English—without having the slightest idea what was actually said! Even worse, imagine the impression his literalism gave his audience of American food and recreational habits! Trying to avoid such error, my search has been for the content of the word rather than its form.

But there have been times when I simply could not catch on to either Paul's words or his ideas, and have had to muddle through as best I could. In these instances I have found myself in perfect agreement with Peter, who said that "our beloved brother Paul, according to the wisdom given unto him, hath written unto you. . . . some things which are hard to be understood" (II Pet. 3:15–16). I was saved from despair only by the knowledge that I was in the company of the first pope.

It may be said that the language of the "cotton patch" version is not elegant, dignified or even nice. Such expressions as "hell, no" and "the damned bastard" might offend those who think of the New Testament characters as dainty saints rather than sweaty men with deep feelings and sensitivities. But Paul may have been exaggerating only slightly when he called himself "the chief of sinners" (I Tim. 1:15). So I have tried to let him be himself, without artificially clothing him with the image of immaculate sainthood. I feel sure that our beloved brother would prefer his "thorn in the flesh," given to him "lest I should be exalted above measure" (II Cor. 12:7), to the fake halo which his would-be admirers insist that he wear.

By the use of these uncouth expressions there has not been the slightest intent to shock, offend or startle—or to please—anyone. But at the same time, no effort has been made to shield the reader from the blunt, vigorous language of these letters.

Nor has consistency been a primary objective. The same Greek word may be translated one way in one passage, a different way in another.

Wherever possible, people's names have been translated rather than transliterated; for example, "Rock" instead of "Peter." At other times they have been simply anglicized, and where this was not feasible, given new names entirely—names of no particular significance.

The place names have been chosen at random, with no particular respect to geography or other relevant details. Thus the letter to "the Christians in Atlanta" may as well have been addressed to Knoxville, Nashville, New Orleans or any other city. The name has no significance other than stage setting. Neither does the American city bear any implied resemblance to the city originally addressed by Paul.

Obviously the "cotton patch" version must not be used as a historical text. The Revised Standard Version and the New English Bible are excellent for this purpose.

Some scholars may object to the inclusion of Ephesians and possibly others as letters from Paul. Since the problems of authorship seem to fall outside the scope of the "cotton patch" approach, I have merely gone along with the traditional *corpus*. I am quite willing to revise the list just as soon as the scholars agree among themselves.

To have lived with Paul during these ardent months of translation has been within itself a fully rewarding experience for me. But if this humble work may be used of God to enlarge and strengthen the faith of others in his Son Jesus Christ, then indeed my joy will be full.

Clarence L. Jordan

Koinonia Farm
Americus, Georgia

The Cotton Patch Version of Paul's Epistles

The Letter to the Christians
in Washington [ROMANS]

1.

1. From Paul, a "captive" of Christ Jesus, an appointed agent assigned to God's great story. It's the story about his Son which God began many years ago in the sacred writings of his spokesmen. This Son, on the human side, was a descendant of David. On the spiritual side he was designated as God's Son by the explosion growing out of the resurrection of the dead. His name is Jesus Christ, our Lord. Through him I got the favor of an appointment to approach, on his behalf, other races, including you all, about faithful obedience on all matters. So you, too, are Jesus Christ's guests.

To everybody in Washington, God's loved ones, his invited guests. Best wishes to you and peace from our Father-God and our Lord Jesus Christ.

8. Let me say first that through Jesus Christ I thank my God for every one of you, because your faithfulness is being reported all over everywhere. God will bear me out on this—the God whom I worship spiritually in the great story of his Son—that I'm continually praying for you all. Every time I pray I ask if somehow it might be God's will for me to have the pleasure of a visit with you folks. For I really am anxious to see you. Maybe I can share some spiritual gift with you that will perk you up. By this I mean that both you and I will be helped by one another's experiences. Now it's no secret, brothers, that many, many times I intended to visit you and still haven't made it. I wanted to pick some of the ripe fruit in your midst as well as in other races. For I have a debt to pay to both Americans and foreigners, to both educated and uneducated. And that's why I have a burning desire to tell the great story to you in Washington. For I am not bashful about the great story, since it is the power of God bringing new life to anyone who takes part in it, whether he be first a white man or a Negro. For in it the curtain is lifted on God's way of goodness, which is lived out by one act of faith after another, just as the script says: "The good man shall live out his faith."

18. It also draws back heaven's curtain on God's displeasure with every form of arrogance and cussedness on the part of men who choke the truth with evil. Knowledge of God is plainly in them, because God himself put it there. For the unseen things about God, such as his everlasting might and his godliness, are clear to anyone who considers all that he did in putting the world together from scratch. So they don't have a leg to stand on. Having this knowledge of God, they neither gave him credit for being God nor thanked him. Rather, they became duds in their sermonizing, and the light of their silly minds went out. Parading themselves as educated, they became little morons and twisted the wonder of the undying God into something resembling a mortal man and flying things, and four-wheeled things and crawlers.

24. That's why God turned them loose in the stink of their planned lusts and let them degrade their own bodies with them. These wise guys swapped God's truth for an outright lie, and then bowed themselves down and worshiped creation rather than the Creator, who is blessed throughout all ages. May it ever be so. That's why, I repeat, God turned them loose in their perverted sex. For their females swapped normal intercourse for abnormal expressions. The males, too, quit the normal intercourse with females and burned in their fever for one another—male with male—practicing the disgrace and having the inevitable results of their perversion show up in their personalities. And since they were not open to having God in their thinking, God turned them loose with a closed mind to act like asses. They are loaded to the gills with every kind of wickedness, evil, greed and meanness. They are stuffed with jealousy, murder, fighting, double-crossing and spite. They are rumor-makers and rumor-circulators, enemies of religion, puffed-up braggarts, blowhards, slick operators, utterly contemptuous of their parents. They are harebrained and unreliable, cold and cruel. And worse, even though they clearly understand God's rule that people who do such things will get the death penalty, they not only keep on doing these things themselves but they buddy up with others who are getting the habit.

2.

1. Now listen here, man—and that includes every preacher—you have nothing to hide behind. For whenever you preach to somebody else, you're laying it on yourself, because you, the preacher, are guilty of the very same things. Yet we are fully aware that *God's truth-packed sermon* is aimed at those who do such things. Now let the man who preaches against others doing certain things when he himself is also doing them consider this: Do you really think that *you'll* be excused from *God's* sermon? And are you turning up your nose at his overflowing kindness and restraint and good humor, forgetting that God's kindness is leading you toward a changed life? By your calloused and unchanged attitude you are piling up on yourself *WRATH*, which God will mete out to each on the basis of his deeds on the Day of Wrath, when God's just laws will be clearly displayed. On the one hand he will give spiritual life to those who, by commitment to the good deed, seek nobility and honor and immortality. On the other hand he will let loose his furious wrath on those who out of self-interest disregard the truth and highly regard the wrong. Hellfire and brimstone upon every son of a gun who works for the wrong, whether he's a "superior" white or a Negro. Nobility and honor and peace to every one who works for the right, whether he's a "superior" white or a Negro. For a man's face cuts no ice with God.

12. So then, those who sinned without the Bible shall also perish without the Bible; and those who sinned with the Bible shall be judged by the Bible.[1] For it is not those who *listen* to Scripture but those who *act* on Scripture that will be considered right with God. So when the people of the world who don't have the Bible act instinctively on things in the Bible, this is the Bible for them, even though they don't have one. They show the *effect* of the Bible written on their hearts. And all along, their conscience is helping them out, explaining and defending issues which arise among them and pointing toward the day when God, through Christ Jesus, will judge the inner lives of people—exactly as I tell the great story.

17. If then you are a white man and you lean back on the Bible and you go all out for God and you know his will and are able to make clear-cut decisions; if you are a good student of the Bible and have reason to believe that you yourself are a qualified leader of the blind, a light to those who are in the dark, an instructor of the unlearned, a teacher of the young; if you have the body of knowledge and truth contained in the Bible—all right, teacher of another, you are teaching yourself, aren't you? You who place such emphasis on the Bible, are you disgracing God by your violations of the Scripture? For it is written, you know, that "it is because of *you* that Christianity is sneered at by non-Christians."

25. Church membership[2] is indeed fine if you live by the Bible; but if you go contrary to the Bible your church membership has turned into paganism. On the other hand, suppose a non-member

---

[1]The word translated "Bible" here is the Greek word for "law" and refers to the religious laws of the Jews contained in the Old Testament. It would therefore mean to them about the same as "Bible" for present-day Christians.

[2]In the Greek the word here means "circumcision." For the Jew it was the initiatory rite ino the household of faith. Since it was the mark of membership in Judaism, its nearest modern counterpart for white Christians is "church membership," or perhaps "baptism" into a white, segregated church.

lives by the ethical precepts of the Bible, will not his non-membership be considered just as good as membership? Then the non-member who instinctively lives up to the Bible will show up you who, with all your Scripture and membership, are a Bible-breaker. For a Christian[3] is not one who makes a show of it, nor is his church membership for status purposes. He is a Christian who is one on the inside, whose membership is of the heart—something spiritual and not mechanical—and who seeks not the approval of society but of God.

3.

1. What's the advantage, then, of being a Christian? Or what's the benefit of church membership? Well, there are all sorts of things. In the first place Christians are trustees of the word of God. All right, so some of them are hypocrites; does their hypocrisy nullify God's sincerity? Hell no.[4] Let God remain true, even if it makes a liar out of every man. To quote the Scriptures:

> ... that you may prove right in all your sayings,
> And have the final word on your day in court.

5. Now suppose that our badness surrenders to God's goodness, then what? Would it then be wrong, humanly speaking, for God to punish us? Why, of course not! Otherwise, how could he judge the world?

7. And if, when I lie, God's truth stands out all the more beautifully, why should I be condemned for lying? Isn't this what others smear us with when they report that we advocate "Let's practice

---

[3]The word is actually "Jew," which, like the word "gentile," seems at times to have purely racial overtones. When this is so we translate it, in the Southern context, "white man," and the word "gentile" as "Negro." At other times these words have primarily religious content, and so we translate the word "Jew" as "Christian" or "church member," and the word "gentile" as "pagan," "non-Christian" or "people of the World," or "the rest of society."

[4]Just about the proper strength for the Greek phrase.

the bad so it will call forth the good." That accusation is utterly ridiculous.

9. So what's the score? Are we church members ahead? Nope, not at all. For I previously pointed out that both church members and non-members alike are all classified under sin, just as the Scripture says,

> There isn't a pure man anywhere,
> Nor one who is fully sensitive.
> Nor one who really sets his heart on God.
> *All* kicked over the traces and became worthless.
> There isn't a one worth his salt,
> Not a single solitary one.

> Their throat is a waiting grave,
> Their tongues are lie factories.
> Behind their lips is the poison of a rattlesnake.
> With their mouths they cuss a blue streak.
> Their feet are spiked to draw blood;
> They leave a trail of broken bones and busted heads,
> And they don't know what peace is.
> Reverence for God is foreign to them.

19. Now we are aware that all the Bible says is directed to those who are committed to it, so as to put a stop to arguing and provide people all over with a standard for obedience to God. And yet no one is put right with God by his relation to the Bible, since the Bible brings only an *awareness* of sin.

21. At the present, then, a right relation with God quite apart from the Bible has become clear. It is spoken of by the Bible itself and by the men of God. I refer to a rightness with God that comes, through Christ's faith, to *all* who put it into practice. It makes no difference *who* it is, since all sinned and flunked out on God's glory.

All, then, are gladly accepted by his kindness expressed through the emancipation granted in Christ Jesus. God accepted him as the full settlement of people's sins when they have faith in his sacrifice. It is a demonstration of God's goodness in showing restraint and overlooking sins done in the past; and it is also a demonstration of his goodness in handling the present situation, showing that he himself is good and that he also makes the person who bases his life on Jesus good.

27. Where, then, is "status" with God? It is locked out. On what grounds? Scriptural ones? No, but on the ground of *faithfulness*. For we consider a person to be made right by his faithfulness, quite apart from his Bible-quoting. Or is God the God of Christians only? Is he not also God of non-Christians? Yes, of non-Christians too, since there is only one God. And he will accept a church member who is faithful as well as a non-church-member who is faithful. Are we then going against the Bible by emphasizing faithfulness? Hell, *no*, we are *establishing* the Bible!

4.

1. Well, then, what am I going to say about the position held by Abraham, the head of our race? For if Abraham was made right by attending services,[5] then he has status, but not with God. For what does the Scripture say? "Abraham put his trust in God, and for him *this* was considered goodness." Now a working man does not consider his paycheck a gift from his employer but the discharge of a debt. But for the man who doesn't put in time and yet is loyal to his employer who makes it right with the idle, his *loyalty* is considered "time." It just like David said when he called a man lucky when God considered him as "making time"[6] without attend-

---

[5] While the word here in the Greek is "works," I take it to mean the kind of "works" or "services" we render God on Sunday morning.

[6] The actual word is "righteousness," or one's loving service to God, one's "divine employment." Hence the figure of putting in "time" in God's service, that is, being "on the job."

ing services. He said:

People are lucky whose charges are dropped and whose violations are scrubbed; Lucky indeed is the man whose boss keeps no account of his errors.

Does this "luckiness" apply to the church member or to the non-church-member? Now we just said that for Abraham *loyalty* was considered as "time." When, then, was it credited to him? After he was baptized or before he was baptized?[7] It was *not* as a baptized man but as an *unbaptized one*. And he accepted the symbol of baptism as an OK on the "time" he got for loyalty before his baptism. Thus he became the daddy of all those whose loyalty before they were baptized was credited to them as "time"; and, the daddy of baptism to those who not only are baptized but who also copy the loyalty of our father Abraham while he was still un-churched.

13. Now the contract with Abraham or his heir that he would be a world figure was not based on church activity but on service which arises from faithfulness. For if only those engaged in church programs are in on the deal, then faithfulness amounts to nothing and the contract is only a scrap of paper. For the church "program"[8] gets God pretty upset. Now where there is no program there is of course no failure to carry it out.

16. The reason that this springs from faithfulness is to establish God's undeserved favor back of the contract with *every* descendant, not only the one in the church program but also the one who shares in Abraham's faithfulness. He is the daddy of us *all*, just as it is written, "I have made you the daddy of *many* different groups." In the light of this, he really did give his loyalty to the God who makes the dead to live and who tells nothing to be something. And he kept the faith even when the cards were stacked

[7]See footnote to 2:25.

[8]Here the word is actually "law" but the emphasis seems to be on "legal activity," that is, the carrying out of the multitude of ecclesiastical rules and regulations, or the "program" of Judaism.

against him. That's how he became "daddy of many other groups," exactly as was said, "Your heir will be such a daddy." Without batting an eye, he faced his own impotence—he was one hundred years old at the time—and the fact that Sarah, his wife, was well beyond her menopause. Still he never concluded that the contract with God had been canceled, but stoutly maintained his faithfulness, giving God credit for being able to carry out *his* end of the bargain. And that's why Abraham "was counted in as being in the swim with God." Now this verse—"he was counted in"—didn't apply just to Abraham, but also to *us* who were yet to be counted in through our faithfulness to him who raised Jesus our Lord from the dead.[9] To bear our sins he was killed; to put us in the swim he was made alive.

5.

1. Since we have been put in the swim with God because of our faithfulness, we have a close relationship with him through our Lord Jesus Christ. Through him we also got an open door into this favored position we hold, and we get "status" from the confidence we receive from God's greatness. Not only so, but we also get "status" for getting banged up, being fully aware that getting banged up makes us tough. Now toughness makes for reliability and reliability for confidence, and confidence doesn't let you down. For God has given us a love transfusion by the Holy Spirit he provided for us. While we were real sick, in the nick of time Christ died for people who couldn't care less for a loving God. Hardly anybody will die for an ordinary person, and it's possible that someone might screw up enough courage to give his life for a truly good person. But God convinces us of *his* love, because *while we were still sinful trash* Christ gave his life for us. So now that

---

[9]Just as the Jews were fleshly descendants of a man who, so far as begetting children was concerned, was "dead," but who by God's grace was rejuvenated—brought back from the "dead"—even so are Christians spiritual descendants of one who was rejuvenated—"raised from the dead." Thus, Jesus is the Christian's Abraham—*a very important point throughout this letter.*

we have been taken on board by his sacrifice, shall we not all the more be saved by him from "the life away from God." For if, while we were rebels, we were won over to God through his Son's death, how much more, having been won over, shall we be saved in his *life*. And on top of all this, we get "status" with God through our Lord Jesus Christ, by whom we have now been won over.

12. All right, now, it's like this: Through one man (Adam) sin got a toehold in the world. Then through sin death got in. And that's how death infected the whole human race and why "everybody sinned." So sin was in the world even before the Bible, but it wasn't chalked up as sin since there was no Bible. Even so, death was king from Adam until the Bible was written, even over those who committed no such sin as did Adam, who is a symbol of what I'm about to explain. Adam's sin, for example, was no match at all for God's generosity. For if many died as the result of the one man's sin, countless thousands more were the beneficiaries of God's kindness and thoughtful generosity bestowed through the one Man Jesus Christ. Nor is the result the same as that of the one who sinned. On the one hand, the result of a single sin was a sentence into exile, while the result of many sins was an unmerited acceptance into favor. If because of one man's disobedient act death became king through that one man, how much more, then, will *life*, through the one Man Jesus Christ, be king over those who accept his bounty of grace and his gift of goodness.

18. Well, then, just as the result of one disobedient act was banishment for the whole human race, even so the result of one God-pleasing act was the restoration to life for the whole human race. For just as the multitudes were lined up as sinners by one man's disobedience, even so will the multitudes be lined up as saints by one Man's obedience. Now Scripture came on the scene to heighten the Fall; but wherever sin flowed, grace overflowed, in order that, as sin was king in the death realm, so might grace, through restoration to favor, be king in the spiritual life realm provided by Jesus Christ our Lord.

6.

1. So what are we advocating? "Let's wallow in sin, so more grace may pour forth"? Hell, no! How can we who *died* in sin still *live* in it? Or are you unaware that we who were initiated into Christ Jesus' fellowship were initiated into *his* death realm? Therefore, through our initiation into the death realm, we are entombed with him, in order that, as Christ was raised from the dead by the Father's glory, so we too might walk in newness of life. For if we have been fellow plants in the garden of his death, we shall also be fellow plants in the garden of his risen life. We are convinced that the person we used to be has been strung up with him, so that the sinful nature may be wiped out, and we no longer need be addicted to sin. For in dying, one is released from sin's claim on him. Yet, if we died with Christ, we believe that we also shall live with him. It is clear that Christ, who was *raised* from the dead, doesn't die any more. Death no longer has a grip on him. As far as sin is concerned he died once and got it over with; but as far as God is concerned, he lives and lives. In the same way we think of ourselves as being dead in relation to sin but very much alive in relation to God in Christ Jesus. Therefore, don't let sin be king of your fragile group, so that it becomes obedient to sin's desires. And don't hand over your members to sin as tools of wickedness, but hand over yourselves to God as people who were dead but are very much alive. Commit your members to God as instruments of justice. Sin shall not lord it over you all, for you are not under compulsion[10] but under kindness.

15. So what about that? Shall we sin just because we're not under compulsion but under kindness? Positively not! Don't you realize that when you hire yourselves out as workers on a job you are duty-bound to carry out the orders of your boss? And this holds true whether you're working for sin on a death job or for obedience

---

[10]The word "law" occurs again here, but this time the emphasis seems to be on the demand of the law, that is, its compulsion.

on a harmony job. But thank God that while you used to be sin's workers you later gave *voluntary* obedience to a type of teaching in which you got carried away. So, having been released from sin's job, you have been employed by goodness. (I'm using a human figure of speech because it's just naturally hard for you to catch on.) All right now, in the same way that you hired out your members as workers in filth and delinquency on the gangster job, so now hire out your members as workers in goodness on the clean-guy job. For when you were sin's workers you owed nothing to goodness. But did you get anything worthwhile out of your job? Just stuff you're now ashamed of—stuff that ends in destruction. But now that you've been released from sin and hired by God, you get your pay for being dedicated, the result of which is spiritual life. For sin's payoff is destruction, but God's reward is spiritual life in Christ Jesus our Lord.

7.

1. You certainly agree, brothers,—and here I'm speaking to those who know their Bibles—that the commandments[11] are binding on a man only during his lifetime. For example, a married woman is legally bound to her husband as long as he lives, but when he dies she is released from her marital vows. If then she sleeps with another man while her husband is still alive, she will be guilty of adultery. But if her husband is dead, she is released from her marital vow and it is not adultery for her to sleep with another man. That's the way it is with you, too, my brothers. Through your membership in Christ's body you were, legally speaking, put to death. Then this freed you to "marry" another —the Risen One—in order that we might raise some *chillun* for God. For before we "died," sin's passions, stimulated by the commandments, made our members pregnant so as to bear children for the death realm. But now that we have "died," we have been

---

[11]Once again the word is "law," but this time the exposed facet is the Mosaic law, or more specifically, the commandments.

released from our marital vow to our former "husband" and are free to remarry in the newness of spiritual life rather than in the old way of legalism.

7. So what are we saying? That the commandments are wrong? Not for a moment. And yet, I would not be *conscious* of wrong if the commandments had not prohibited it. For example, I would not have been conscious of lusting for things if the commandments had not said, "You shall not lust for things." Then sin, taking advantage of the commandment, worked up in me every conceivable lust for things. So without a prohibition, sin is inoperative.[12] Now let's suppose that I were living without any legal code. Then some prohibition came along and sin seized on it and killed me. Then, in a sense, the prohibition, which was supposed to help me live, became the occasion of my death. For sin took advantage of the prohibition, made an ass of me and then slew me with it. This was in spite of the fact that there's nothing wrong with the law itself nor the specific commandment, which is just and fair.

13. Did something *good*, then, bring about my destruction? I should say not! Rather, it was sin—naked sin—*working through a good thing*, that destroyed me. So then sin, working through the commandment, became the biggest sinner of all. Now we all recognize that the commandments are spiritual, but I'm not. I'm human, bought off by sin. Half the time I don't know which end is up. The things I really don't want I make a habit of, and the things I just despise I go right on doing. But when I say that I go right on doing what *I* don't want, then I'm agreeing with the Bible that *it* has a good point (in prohibiting it). Actually, then, it isn't even *I* who commit the act but the *sinful habit* to which I'm addicted. I know full well that from a human standpoint the element of good is not at work in me. The *desire* to do right is there, yes, but the deed, no. I simply don't carry through on my good intentions; worse, I fall into the habit of doing the bad things I *don't* intend. If then I keep on doing things *against* my will, it really isn't I, is

---

[12]That is, in the absence of a prohibition there cannot be a violation.

it, who's committing the act but the sinful habit that's in my driver's seat. I am discovering the principle that when I really want to do right, wrong embraces me. Way down deep inside of me I appreciate God's law, but I'm seeing a different "law" at work in my personality—a law which violently wars against my better judgment and takes me prisoner to the sinful addictions of my personality. What a scoundrel I am! Who can get me out of this rut of destruction? Thank God, it is done through Jesus Christ our Lord.

25. So now you see that intellectually I bind myself to the law of God, but down where I actually live, to the law of sin.

8.

1. There is, then, no charge outstanding against those who are in (wedlock to) Jesus Christ. For the Spirit's law of new life in Christ Jesus released you from the claims of the law of sin and destruction. For when it became clear that legalism was a failure, due to its weakness in dealing with humanity, God sent his own Son, in an exact replica of a man of sin and for sin, and dealt effectively with human sin. He did this in order that the just aims of the commandments might be realized in us who live not on the level of man but on the level of the Spirit. For they who are man-centered think along human lines, and they who are Spirit-centered think in terms of the Spirit. For man-centered reasoning deadends in destruction, but Spirit-centered reasoning leads to life and space. Man-centered reasoning is hostile to God, because it does not subordinate itself to God's plan nor indeed can it do so. People who are man-centered just can't get along with God. But you all, you are not man-centered but Spirit-centered—provided, of course, that God's Spirit permeates you. If one doesn't have Christ's spirit, he isn't Christ's man. But if Christ *is* in you, the self, because of its sin, is stone dead; but the Spirit, because it is good, is throbbing with life. And if the Spirit of the God who made Jesus to live again permeates you, then this same God will also give life to your hellbent egos by means of his Spirit that permeates you.

12. It's a fact, then, brothers, that we are under no obligation whatsoever to live a man-centered life. If you do live that way, you're gonna blow yourselves to smithereens. Yet if by the Spirit you utterly smash your selfishness, you will live. For God's sons are they who are led by *God's* Spirit.

15. Listen, you all didn't get an old master-slave relationship based on fear; instead, you got a father-son relationship in which we are entitled to call God *"Father."* The Spirit himself sings out with our spirit that "WE ARE GOD'S CHILDREN." And if we are his children, we are also his heirs. If, indeed, we are his heirs, then we are Christ's fellow-heirs—provided, of course, that we identify with his suffering in order to join in his reward. For I figure that the sufferings we are enduring can't hold a candle to the splendor that's going to become evident in us. In fact, the fondest dream of the universe is to catch a glimpse of real live sons of God. For the universe is in the grip of futility—not voluntarily, but because someone got control of it—and it is hoping against hope that it will be emancipated from the slavery of corruptness into the marvelous freedom of being the *children* of God. For we know that the whole world is agonizing and hurting up to the very present. And not just it, but we ourselves as we anticipate sonship, which means the liberation of our group. In fact, it was our *hope* that got us by. Now hope isn't expecting something you already see, because when one *sees* something, how can he *hope* for it? But if we hope for what we don't see, then it takes patience to wait for it.

26. Similarly, the spirit also helps us out in our weakness. For example, we don't know beans about praying, but the Spirit himself speaks up for our unexpressed concerns. And he who X-rays our hearts understands the Spirit's approach, since the Spirit represents Christians before God.

28. We are convinced that God fully cooperates in a good cause with those who love him and who are chosen for his purpose. He has known such people before, and he set them forth, shaping them into the exact image of his Son, who thus became the first boy in a whole line of brothers. It's these whom he set forth that he also invited, and the ones he invited he accepted into fellowship. And it's these whom he accepted into fellowship that he equipped with credentials.

31. How, then, shall we respond to all this? If God is rootin' for us, who can win over us? If he didn't hold back his own Son, but put him in the game for us all, won't he even more gladly, in addition to his Son, equip us with all we need to win the game?

33. Who shall reject us when God has elected us? God *accepts* us into fellowship; who banishes us? Does Christ Jesus, the Killed One, or rather, the Risen One, who is God's "right-hand man" and speaks out for us? What shall drive a wedge between us and the love of Christ? Shall trouble or hardship or persecution or drought or poverty or danger or war? It's as the Scripture says:

> For your sake we face death throughout the day;
> We are thought of as slaughterhouse sheep.

And yet—and yet—*we come out on top everytime through him who set his heart on us.* For I am absolutely convinced that neither death nor life, nor angels nor rulers nor the present nor the future nor force nor mountain nor valley nor anything else in the universe shall be able to separate us from the love of God which is in Christ Jesus our Lord.

9.

1. As a Christian who doesn't lie and whose conscience is examined by the Holy Spirit, I'm telling you the honest truth: In my heart there is great grief and steady pain. For I would be willing to sacrifice even my own life in Christ for the sake of my native white American Protestant brethren.[13] They are "good white folks"; they are "saved"; they have prestige; they have the Bible; they have a denominational program; they have worship services and Sunday schools; they have theological doctrines and are staunch supporters of Christ himself. And God, who is over them all, is unceasingly magnified. So be it. But it was not for the likes of this that the word of God has come raining down. For not all Protestants are Protestants, and not all "good white folks" are *good* white folks. Rather, "your line shall be perpetuated through *Isaac*."[14] This means that God's people are not the ones who give that appearance but whose *lives* are rooted in God's promises. Now this is how the promise was stated: "I'll come at the proper time and give Sarah a son." Not only this, but when Rebecca was pregnant by our father Isaac, she was told, "The first shall serve the last." This was said even before the twins had been born or had done anything either good or bad, which shows that God's program of choice rests not on man's deeds but on God himself. It's just as the Scripture says, "*I* loved Isaac and *I* rejected Esau."

14. Well then, what do we say about this? Does this make God unfair? Not at all. For he says in the Old Testament,

> *I'll* show mercy when *I* show mercy,
> And *I'll* show compassion when *I* show compassion.

---

[13]There is no intent whatsoever on the part of the translator to single out Protestants above any other Christian group. Since Paul was an ex-Pharisee, and the Pharisees were the predominant sect of Judaism, we have brought him over into the modern times of "cotton patch" perspective as a white, American ex-Protestant, since this group predominates in the United States, particularly in the Southern region.

[14]It is practically impossible to translate this passage into modern equivalents. What Paul is saying here is that there are *two* streams of Judaism, both stemming from Abraham. But one was in the covenant relationship and the other was not. Thus, while both lines claimed to be true Jews (white American Protestants), not all of them were.

So then, the mercy doesn't come from the one who wants it, nor from the one who runs after it, but from God himself. Also, in the Scripture God says to Pharaoh, "The reason I brought you on the scene was to display my power through you and to use you to spread news of me throughout the whole world." So then, *he* decides who gets mercy and who gets the works.

19. All right, you will say to me, "If *he* calls the signals, why does he still hold *us* responsible? Who ever really goes contrary to his plan when *he* does all the driving?" My dear fellow, you wouldn't be giving God any sass, would you? Does the design say to the designer, "Why did you make me like this?" Or doesn't the potter have the right to make his lump of clay into either an expensive vase or an everyday pot? Then what's wrong if God wants to exercise his displeasure or assert his authority? Suppose he has a vase that's already marked for the junkpile and he works it over very carefully just to show his marvelous skill to a favorite vase he made earlier for display. Isn't that OK? Indeed, *we* are that junkpile vase, and he has assembled us not only from among church members but also from among the people in the street. It's as it says in Hosea,

> I will assemble a people who aren't my people,
> And the *unloved* into a Beloved Community;
> And it shall be that on the spot where it was said to them,
> "You folks, you're not God's people,"
> Right there they shall be called sons of the *Living* God.

And Isaiah cries out regarding white American Protestants,[15]

> Even though the WAP's[16] outnumber the sand of the seas, it's *those that are left* that shall be saved. For the Lord, push-

---

[15]See footnote, verse 3. The word here, as well as in verse 3, is actually "Israel," which refers to Judaism both racially and religiously.

[16]White American Protestants.

ing things to a conclusion and cutting off debate, will make a settlement on the earth.

Again, it's as Isaiah foretold it:

If the Lord of peace had not left us a germ of life,
We would have wound up like Hiroshima, and would have
been treated like Nagasaki.

30. So what are we saying? Simply this: that the unchurched people, who didn't even try to get religion, *did* get religion—religion based on *action*.[17] And yet the WAP's, trying so hard at Bible religion, never quite caught on to the Bible. Why not? Because they were not people of faithful action but of religious activities. They ground themselves down on the grindstone, just as the Scripture says,

Look, I'm setting up in Protestantism a grindstone, a rock of
danger,
And he who follows the instructions for it won't be ground
down.

10.

1. Brothers, my heart's desire and my prayer to God is for their deliverance. For I can vouch for them that they do have enthusiasm for God, but it isn't enlightened. Not understanding God's program, and trying to set up one of their own, they didn't yield to *God's* program. For Christ puts the Bible in focus on a program for every one who lives his faith. Now the Old Testament says that the man who commits himself to the Bible program shall live by it. But the faith program puts it this way: "Don't say to yourself, 'Who'll climb the sky [that is, to bring down God's Anointed One]?' or, 'Who'll descend into the afterlife [that is, to

---

[17] While the word here is literally "faith," it means to believe strongly enough in something to *act* on it.

bring back God's anointed one from the realm of the departed] ?' "
But what does it say? "The word is already present with you"—
in what you say and believe. By "the word" is meant the doctrine
of faithfulness which we are spreading. Because if you come out
in the open and say, "Jesus is Lord,"[18] and if you believe deep
down in your heart that God raised him from the dead, you shall
be saved. For by one's heart one is activated into God's program,
and by one's mouth one makes the public declaration into salvation. For the Scripture says: "Everyone who follows the instructions for it won't be ground down." There just isn't any distinction
made between the WAP and the man in the street. God himself is
Lord over *all* and leans over backward toward *all* who join his
movement. For the Scripture says, "Everyone who takes upon himself the Lord's name[19] shall be saved."

14. How, then, shall they join one's movement without having
confidence in him? And how shall they have confidence in someone they've never heard of? And how shall they hear about him
without someone to spread the news? And how shall they spread
the news unless they have the facts? As the Scripture says, "How
beautiful are the feet of those who bring good news that's sound."

16. But, not all responded obediently to the great story. Isaiah
says, "Lord, who put any stock in our report?" Now confidence
arises from the report, and the report is based on Christ's word.
But I raise the question, "Was it that they just didn't hear?" No,
indeed.

> The drumbeat of these things went out over the whole earth,
> and the newscasts of them into every corner of civilization.

So I ask, *"Didn't white American Protestants know?"*

---

[18]This was the affirmation which Christians made to government authorities
who demanded of them supreme loyalty to the state and to so indicate it by
publicly declaring, "Caesar Is Lord."

[19]To call one's self, or take, another's name meant to identify with him
and support his cause or ideas as a follower or disciple. Thus, one "takes
Christ's name" by joining the Christian movement.

19. To begin with, the Old Testament says,

I'll stir you to action with a nation that isn't Christian; I'll get you riled up with a nation that's gone cuckoo.

And even Isaiah dared to say:

I was discovered by people who weren't even looking for me; I became clear to those who didn't argue about me.

Then he refers to the WAP's:

Throughout the livelong day I tried to shake hands with a disobedient and impudent people.

11.

1. I ask, therefore, "Has God walked out on his people?" Absolutely not. For I myself am also a WAP—a pure Anglo-Saxon and a Baptist. God has *not* walked out on his people whom he knew from way back. Don't you remember the story of Elijah, how he made a case against the WAP's before God? He said, "Lord, they've killed your preachers; they've desecrated your pulpits, and I'm the only one left—and they're gunning for me!" But what does the divine correction say to him? "I still have left for my own use seven thousand men who haven't compromised with the sex-and-money cult." Similarly, then, there is at the present time a small minority which has been selected by God's grace. Now if it is by God's grace, then it isn't the result of man's activity; if so, grace wouldn't be "grace" at all.

7. So now what? Precisely this: White American Protestantism hasn't achieved its goal. However, the "selected fraction" got through, while all the rest were calloused. This Scripture describes them:

God gave them a sleepy spirit,
Eyes that don't look, and ears that don't listen,
Right up to the present day.

35

And David puts it this way:

> May their communion table become for them a slick trick and
> a hoax,
> An invitation to delusion and a frame-up.
> May their eyes be blinded so they don't see;
> And forever break their backs!

11. So I ask, "Does the fact that they stumped their toe mean that they fell flat on their face?" Not at all. Rather, because of their failure the Christian faith went to the unchurched, so as to get the WAP's on the ball. Now if their *failure* benefited the outside world, and their negligence benefited the unchurched, how much more would their success!

13. Now I have a few words for you "outsiders." Since I myself am an agent of Christ to the outsiders, I take this responsibility very seriously, with the hope that I may stir my brothers to action and save some of them. For if their exclusion meant the inclusion of the outside world, what will their acceptance mean, if not life from death itself? Now if the sample is OK, so is the whole batch. And if the root is true, so are the branches. But if the tree is top-worked, and you, a bud from another tree, are grafted in with the other shoots and share the root and sap of the stock, don't you turn up your nose at the other shoots. If you do turn up your nose, just remember that *you* don't nourish the stock; *it* nourishes you.

19. But you will say, "Yeah, but the branches were pruned off, so I could be grafted in." All right, *why* were they pruned? Because they weren't true. And why were *you* grafted in? Only because *you stood the test.* Don't throw your head so high in the air; instead, tremble in your boots. For if God didn't spare the shears on the natural branches, will he spare them on you? Consider, then, *both* the gentleness of God's graft and the sharpness of his shears—sharpness on those who let God down, and gentleness on you, provided of course, you live within the framework of his gentleness. Otherwise, he'll prune you off too. By the same token, if they stop living in their unfaithful position, they will be grafted into the stock, for God himself is able to do the regrafting. For if you, a bud growing naturally on another tree, were cut out and grafted, against nature, into this stock, how much more will the natural buds be grafted into their own parent stock?

25. I don't want you, brothers, to be unaware of the deeper meaning lying hidden in all this, lest you jump to your own conclusions. It's simply this: the callousness that has come over most of white American Protestantism will last only until the idea of the full equality of other groups is established. In this case, of course, the whole of white American Protestantism will be saved. As the Scripture says,

> From the church will arise the Leader;
> He'll wean Christendom of its godlessness.
> And this will be the contract I'll make with them
> When I scrub out their sins.

True, the gospel shows them up as "enemies" for your sakes, but God's selective service act classifies them as "beloved sons" on account of their heritage. For God's considerations and classifications are not subject to review. For just as you used to disobey God, and now, while they are still disobedient, you have been pardoned, even so they, though disobedient now during your time of mercy, may be pardoned later on. God just lumped the whole works together as disobedient, so that he might start with everybody on the basis of mercy.

33. Man, oh man, what a mine of wealth, wisdom and knowledge God has! And his decisions—beyond comprehension; his actions—unexplorable!

> Who ever probed the Lord's mind?
> Or who became his psychiatrist?
> Or who made him a loan
> And it shall be fully repaid.

Everything comes from him, passes through him and goes to him. To him, then, be the credit into the ages. Please may it be so.

12.

1. And so, my brothers, with God's tenderness I am pleading with you to dedicate your whole selves to God as a proper, holy, living sacrifice, for this is your logical act of worship. And don't let the present age keep you in its cocoon. Instead, metamorphose into the new mind, so as to be capable of discerning God's design, which is good and right and mature.

3. As one who has himself been given undeserved favor, I advise every last one of you not to overestimate his importance. Rather, let each estimate wisely according to the portion of faith which God distributed to him. For although one body has many parts, not all the parts have the same function. And so it is with us Christians. Though many, we are one body, with each one a part of the others. We have talents which vary according to the undeserved favor bestowed upon us. If your talent is preaching, use it for the explanation of the faith; if it's hopping tables, use it for hopping tables; if it's teaching, use it for teaching; or if it's counseling, use it for counseling. Let the treasurer perform with honesty, the superintendent with diligence, and the benevolence chairman with cheerfulness. Love has no false face. Shun evil, hang on to good. I mean:

—in brotherliness, showing genuine concern for one another;
—in courtesy, putting others above yourselves;`
—in enthusiasm, never letting up;
—in morale, glowing;
—in the Lord's work, slaving;
—in hope, bubbling over;
—in trouble, taking it;
—in prayer, keeping it up;

—in meeting needs of church members, sharing;
—in hospitality, going out of your way.

14. Bless those who do you in. Bless them, I say, and don't cuss them. Join in the fun with those having fun; join in the tears with those shedding tears. Treat each other equally; pay no special attention to the upper crust, but mingle freely with the lower class people. And don't scratch each other's back. Never return evil for evil. Have respect for things which everybody else considers worthwhile. If it's possible—that is, from your side—WAGE PEACE WITH ALL MANKIND. Don't take vengeance into your own hands, my dear ones, but rather make room for another's wrath. For the Bible says,

> "Revenge is *my* job," says the Lord,
> "*I* will tend to it."

But if your enemy hungers, bread him; if he thirsts, water him. In this way you'll fill his noggin with lighted charcoal. Don't be overwhelmed by evil, but overwhelm evil with good.

13.

1. Let *every human being* submit himself to the Supreme Powers. For there is no power except from God, and the existing ones have been set up by God. The person who resists the power, then, is opposing God's arrangement. And they who have resisted will get a sentence on themselves.

3. Rulers are no fear when the deed is good but when it is bad. You don't want to be afraid of the law? Do good and you'll have its praise, for it is, for you, God's instrument to accomplish good. But if you do wrong, watch out, because he doesn't pack that pistol for nothing. He is God's agent, a warden responsible to society for the one engaging in crime. Therefore it is obligatory that you submit, not only for the sake of society[20] but conscience. For the same reason you are to pay your taxes. For even tax collectors are God's servants, too, to carry on the same purposes. Pay up all your creditors; pay tax to the tax collector, toll to the toll collector, fear to the fear collector, honor to the honor collector! In fact, don't owe anybody anything but love! For the man who loves his neighbor has more than kept the law. "Don't sleep with someone you're not married to, don't murder, don't steal, don't lust for things," and every other commandment are all summed up in this simple one: "Love your neighbor as yourself." Love never does a neighbor harm. It gives flesh and blood to the law.

11. And remember that this is *"The Day."* It's time already for you to get out of bed, because the salvation we have is much nearer to acceptance than when *we* put our trust in it. The night is fading; the day is dawning. So let's take off our pajamas and put on our work clothes. Let's live as becomes the day—not in wild parties and drunkenness, not in jumping into beds and in sex orgies, not in bickering and jealousy. Instead, clothe yourselves with the Lord Jesus Christ, and make no plan for using the body for lust.

14.

1. Accept a brother whose faith is immature, but don't get into a hassle with him over petty points. While one person believes it's all right to eat anything, an immature person might eat only vegetables. Well, don't let the man who eats something look down

---

[20]The word which we translate "society" here is literally "the wrath." As in other places in Paul's letters it seems to refer to the whole human structure which God has allowed rebellious man to build in an effort to order his life quite apart from God. Though God is highly displeased with this godless, man-made order, or society, he still is interested in and concerned for it. So while God does not *will* this order, he does permit it, and therefore its officers and rulers may be considered his "agents." His love still wishes no evil to this "child of wrath," but longs for its ultimate redemption.

his nose at someone who won't, and don't let the guy who doesn't eat a thing damn the person who does. For *God* has accepted the man you reject. You, there, who are you to pass on another man's worker? Whether he's a success or failure is up to his own boss. (But he'll be a success, because the Boss is able to make a success of him.)

5. Now here's a fellow who decides that a certain day is more important than another, and there's a man who decides they're all alike. All right, let each one make up his own mind about it. For he who observes a certain day, observes it in the Lord's presence and he who eats does so in the Lord's presence, since he thanks God for it. Also, he who doesn't eat refrains in the Lord's presence and he too thanks God for this. For not a one of us lives all to himself. For if we live, we live in the Lord's presence, and if we die, we die in the Lord's presence. This is why Christ died and lived, that he might be Lord of both dead people and live ones. So you, now, why do you pass on your brother? And you over there, why are you so snooty towards your brother? For *we all* shall stand up before God's bar, just as the Scripture says:

"As sure as I live," says the Lord, "every soul will get down on his knees before me, and every man's tongue will admit that I'm God."

So then, each of us will account for *himself* before God.

13. Then let's quit rating each other. Rather, you test yourselves on this: "I do not put an obstacle or a trap in front of my brother."

14. I know and am convinced beyond all doubt that from the Christian viewpoint no external thing is of itself wrong, except something which is considered wrong by another. From *his* standpoint it is wrong. So, if your brother is grieved by your food habits, you are no longer walking the way of love. Don't destroy, with your food habits, a person for whom Christ *died*. Therefore, don't let the good name of you all be ridiculed, for the God movement is not doughnuts and coffee, but justice and peace and joyfulness in the Holy Spirit. He who puts his Christian service on this basis is pleasing to God and trustworthy to men.

19. In the light of this, let's go all out for the things of peace and the things that strengthen our life together. Do not tear up God's work for the sake of a food habit. Everything external is quite all right; but the evil is through the *obstacle* set up by a person with this view. It is fine indeed not to eat ham or drink wine or do anything else for your brother to stump his toe on. You just hang onto the faith which you have between yourself and God. A man who doesn't have to grade *himself* on the test is lucky. But he who straddles the fence on the issue of eating is in a bad way, since his position is not one of conviction. And it's a sin when you have no conviction on anything.

15.

1. We mature Christians ought to help the immature ones over their rough spots and not try to make an easy go of it just for ourselves. Let each of us make it easy for our neighbor to get along well in the church community. For Christ didn't put his interests first, but he did as the Scripture says: "The spit of those spitting at you hit *me*." (By the way, all these things that were written down a long time ago were actually written for our instruction too, that we might get inspiration through the endurance and encouragement pictured there.)

5. May the God of endurance and encouragement grant that you treat each other equally according to the Christian faith, so that as one body with one mouth you might praise the God and Father of our Lord Jesus Christ.

7. Therefore, you all accept one another just as Christ also accepted us, to God's glory. For I claim that Christ became a servant of the white religious establishment for the sake of God's truth, so as to make good on his assurances to the church reformers. But for those *outside* the white establishment, he did it out of sheer joy, as the Scripture puts it:

That's why I'll testify with the outsiders and join them in hymns to your name.

And again it says:

Share the joy, you outsiders, with his people.

And again,

Praise the Lord, all you outsiders;
Let *all* people praise him together.

And again Isaiah says,

It shall be that a white Protestant will be raised up to lead the outsiders, and they'll pin their hopes on him.

May the God of hope load you up with every kind of joy and peace in your life of faith, so that with the help of the Holy Spirit you may be running over with confidence.

14. As far as I myself am concerned, my brothers, I am fully convinced that you all are full of goodness, well rounded out with much knowledge, and that you are able to straighten out one another. On some matters, though, I've written quite strongly to you. So you must keep in mind the undeserved favor granted to me from God, that is, that I am Christ Jesus' priest to those who are *not* WAP's. I am organizing *them* along the lines of God's great story, so that what they are setting up may be acceptable and that it may be approved by the Holy Spirit. So then, I do have status in the Christian faith for performing God's work. I won't dare mention anything except what Christ has done through me to convert the non-WAP's. By word and deed, by power shown in signs and miracles, and by spiritual power I have put flesh on Christ's great story from Charleston to Little Rock. Likewise, I consider it a special privilege to tell the story where people never saw a live Christian before, lest I get credit for someone's else's spadework. Instead, it's as the verse which says:

> They who didn't get the word about him shall see,
> And they who never really heard will get the point.

22. It is for this reason that I have often been prevented from visiting you. But now, since I can't find any more virgin territory in these parts, and since I've had for several years a deep longing to visit you, I'll try to make it when I go to Maine. I do hope to see you on my way through, and when I've been filled in on various details by you all, I'd appreciate some help from you on my travel expenses.

25. Right now, however, I'm heading for Charleston with some funds for the church members there. For the Mississippi and Louisiana churches voted to raise a certain sum for the hard-up members in Charleston. I said they voted; actually they *owed* it, because if the white Christians shared their spiritual things with the Negro Christians, the latter are morally obligated to share their material things with their white brothers. So when I've wound up this job and have a signed receipt from them for the full amount, I'll set out for Maine via Washington. And I'm sure that as I travel to you I'll come with Christ's full blessing.

30. And now, my brothers, by our Lord Jesus Christ and by the love of the Spirit, I beg you please to agonize with me and for me in your prayers to God. Pray that I may not fall into the hands of un-Christian people in South Carolina and that my service in Charleston might meet with the approval of the Christians there. Then my journey to you will be a happy one, and with God's permission I'll relax a while with you. May the God of peace please be with you all.

16.

1. I highly recommend to you our sister Phoebe, who is a minister of material things in the Memphis church. I ask that you receive her as a full member of the fellowship and that you lend her a hand in whatever way she may need you, for she herself has a reputation for helping others—including myself.

3. Say hello to Prissy and Adrian, my co-workers for Christ Jesus. They stuck their necks out to save my life, and for this not only am I thankful but all the Negro churches as well. Greetings also to the church that meets in their home. Hello to my dear Ellwood, who was the first real Christian in Alabama. And hello to Mary, who worked so hard for you. Warm regards to Andy and Junior, my kinfolks and fellow captives, who are highly respected in ministerial circles. Best wishes to Ansley, so dear to me in the Lord. Greetings to Howard, our Christian co-worker, and my dear Stocky. Regards to Everett, a true Christian. Say hello to the Harris Baker family. Hello, Cousin Helena. Hello to the faithful Nicholson family. Greetings to Truman and Trudy, the Lord's workers. Say hello to dear Pearl, a hard worker for the Lord if ever there was one. Remember me to Rufus, a prince of a Christian, and to his mother—and mine. Give my love to Austin, Phil, Herb, Perry, Herman and the brothers with them. Much love to Frank and Julia, and to Maro and his sister, and to Ollie and all the other Christians with them. Give everybody a big hug. All of Christ's churches greet you.

17. I warn you, brothers, keep your eye peeled for those who make sects and scandals by going against the training you received. Shun them like the plague, for such gentlemen are not committed to our Lord Christ but to their own welfare. With their smooth sermons and pious prayers they captivate the minds of the immature. For news of your unswerving obedience has spread all over, and so I'm quite happy over you all. Yet I want you to be geniuses at goodness but duds at deviltry. The God of peace will shortly squash the Devil under your feet. May the undeserved favor of our Lord Jesus be with you all.

21. My co-worker Timothy sends his regards, as do my cousins Lou, Jake and Daddy-boy. (I, Terry, the stenographer for this letter, greet you all in the Lord.) Garry, host to me and the whole fellowship, wants to be remembered to you. Hank, the city treasurer, and Brother Charles send their greetings.

25. And now, praise forevermore to him who has the power to shape you up according to my Great Story and the message of Jesus Christ, according to the unveiling of the secret which was locked up for ages but which now, by Eternal God's order, has been opened up through prophetic writings and made known to all the races for their obedience to the faith! Praise forevermore, I say, to the only wise God, through Jesus Christ. Amen.

Paul

A Letter to the Christians in Atlanta [I CORINTHIANS]

1.

1. Paul, summoned into the ministry of Jesus Christ by God's will, and Brother Sam, to God's people in Atlanta—those whom Jesus Christ has set apart by calling them together—who under all circumstances identify themselves with Jesus Christ as their Lord—yes, theirs and ours too—grace and peace to you from our Father-God and from the Lord Jesus Christ.

4. I am continually thanking God for the wonderful thing he did for you in giving you Christ Jesus, who has enriched you in so many ways. This is evident in both your conversation and your understanding. As a matter of fact, the Christian testimony has been thoroughly implanted in you so that you might not lack any spiritual gift and may be really eager for a clearer view of our Lord Jesus Christ. Indeed, he will stand by you, come what may. Furthermore, you won't have a guilty feeling in the presence of our Lord Jesus Christ. You can truly rely upon God, who has called you together into the community *(koinonia)* of his Son, Jesus Christ our Lord.

10. Now brothers, in the name of our Lord Jesus Christ, I call upon every one of you to be in unity with the rest of your brothers. Let there be no splits in your ranks, but rather be knit together in singleness of mind and purpose. I'm saying this, my brothers, because some friends of Clara's reported to me that there were factions springing up among you. To be specific, various ones of you are saying, "I'm on Paul's side," "I'm on Oliver's side," "I'm on Rock's side," "I'm on *Jesus'* side." Tell me this, since when did Christ get so split up? And was *Paul* lynched for you? Or were you given *Paul's* name when you were initiated? I'm really thankful that I didn't initiate a single one of you—except Cris and Garry —so no one has a right to claim that he was given my name at his initiation. (Oh, yes, I forgot, I did initiate Stephen's family, but other than that I don't recall initiating anyone else.) The fact is, Christ didn't appoint me merely to initiate converts, but to tell the great story, simply and without display of learning, lest the noose of Christ become something to be toyed with.

18. To the so-called "practical" people, the idea of the noose is a lot of silly talk, but to those of us who have been let in on its meaning, it is the source of divine power. It's just like the Scripture says:

I will tear to bits the dissertations of the Ph.D.s;
I will pull the rug from under those who have all the answers.

Then what becomes of the "bright" boy? What does this do to the "egghead"? Where does the worldly-wise professor wind up? Hasn't God made human reasoning appear utterly ridiculous? Therefore, since the world with all of its learning was unable to understand God, God in his own wisdom decided to save, through the "folly" of the Christian message, all those who put their trust in it. So, while the church people are always demanding some miraculous display and the scientists are looking for intellectual answers, we go right on proclaiming a *lynched* Christ.[1] To be sure,

---

[1]It may be that "lynched" is not a good translation of the Greek word which means "crucified." Christ was legally tried, if we may call it that, and officially condemned to death. So, technically speaking, it was not a lynching. But anyone who has watched the operation of Southern justice at times knows that more men have been lynched by "legal" action than by night-riding mobs. Pilate publicly admitted that his prisoner was being lynched when he called for a basin and washed his hands of official responsibility. If modern judges were as honest, then "lynching" would be an appropriate translation of "crucifixion."

this is an insult to some churchmen, and so much bunk to the non-Christians, but to those in the fellowship, whether they are churchmen or scientists, white or black, Christ is God's power and God's wisdom. And bear in mind that God's "foolishness" is far superior to human wisdom, and that God's "weakness" is stronger than man's might.

26. Now take a look at your fellowship, brothers. Very few of your members are highly educated, not many are influential or from the upper crust. It appears as though God deliberately selected the world's "morons" to show up the wise guys, and the world's weaklings to show up the high and mighty, and the world's lowly and rejected—the nobodies—to put the heat on the somebodies. So then no human being should puff himself up in the presence of God. Actually, it is for him that you yourselves are in Christ Jesus, who for us is wisdom and righteousness and dedication and redemption—all of it straight from God. That's why the Scripture says, "If you simply must brag, give the credit to the Lord."

2.

1. Now brothers, while I was with you, I did not go around preaching God's word with a lot of fancy sermons or learned discourses. For I had decided to concentrate all my attention on Jesus Christ (and a *lynched* man at that!). You know how weak I was, how fearful (often I actually trembled), and that my talks and sermons did not consist of witty, captivating phrases, but of an actual demonstration of the Spirit's power, so that your faith might not be grounded in human reasoning but in God's strength.

6. On the other hand, the more mature ones among us do discuss education, or "wisdom," but it is not the kind which is being presently emphasized or which is so valued in the higher circles of superficial learning. Rather, we refer to God's wisdom as a kind of mystery, or secret, which God has kept since the beginning of time for our enlightenment. It is something which the present-day officials never seemed to grasp, for if they had, they obviously would not have permitted such a wonderful fellow to be lynched. Here is what the Scriptures say:

> No eye has seen, no ear has heard,
> No human heart has grasped
> The wondrous things which God himself
> Has shown to those who love him.

10. Now it was through the Spirit that God made these things known to us. For the Spirit penetrates everything, even to the very depths of God. Let's look at it this way: Can anybody else really know your own heart like your own spirit? All right, then, can anybody else know God's own heart like his own Spirit? Certainly not, and that's why we were not given the spirit of the world, but the Spirit of God to help us understand the things which he has so freely turned over to us.

13. What I'm trying to say is that this instruction is not the result of education on the human level, but rather it comes from the Spirit's teaching; that is, we use spiritual insights to ascertain spiritual truths. For example, a man with a secular background finds it difficult to understand things from a spiritual point of view, for it is all foolishness to him. He just can't grasp it, because it is in spiritual language. On the other hand, the man with a spiritual experience grasps it readily without help from anyone. But even so, who ever fully knows the Lord's mind? Who can really carry on a conversation with him? Yet, *we* have Christ's mind!

3.

1. Now my brothers, I was unable to speak to you as spiritually mature persons, but rather I had to think of you as quite ordinary people—*babies* in Christ. I gave you a bottle, not solid food. That's all you could take. And you still don't seem to be doing much better, because you are just as material-minded as ever. For when there is jealousy and bickering among you, aren't you behaving like any ordinary human beings? And when you start crowing, "I'm a *Paul* man," and somebody else yells, "I'm for Oliver!" aren't you pathetically human. Wait a minute. Who is Oliver anyway? And who *is* Paul? Both are simply the *servants* who brought the gospel to you, who performed each his duty in his own way as the Lord wished it. I planted, Oliver cultivated, but God made the crop grow. So it makes little difference who plants or who cultivates, but *who makes it grow*. Both the planter and the cultivator are the same, and each shall be paid on the basis of his work. Oliver and I are God's hired hands and you all are his farm, his "mansion," so to speak. Like a skilled craftsman, and using all my God-given insights, I laid out the foundation, and then left it to others to put up the building. Now let everybody be careful how he builds, for he cannot redo the existing foundation, which is Jesus Christ. So if anyone puts up a building on this foundation, whether it be of gold, silver, expensive stone, lumber, straw or twigs, it shall obviously be his own work, standing out as clear as day, as though it were spotlighted. And the test of every man's work will be whether or not it can stand the spotlight. If it can, then of course he'll be "paid off." But if it can't then he'll lose everything he has in it, even though he himself might manage to scrape by. Aren't you all aware that you are God's "mansion" in which God's spirit lives? And if anybody messes up God's house, God will mess him up. For God's house (and that includes every one of you) is indeed a sacred thing.

18. Let nobody kid himself; if anyone gets the idea that he is worldly-wise let him become an idiot so that he might be truly wise. For worldly wisdom is idiocy before God, just as it is written, "He caught the intellectuals in their own trap." And again, "The Lord knows that intellectual discussions are vain." So, let nobody brag about human accomplishments. In reality, you own everything—Paul, Oliver, Rock, the world, life, death, the present, the future—everything. And you belong to Christ, and Christ to God.

4.

1. Please consider us as Christ's assistants and as trustees of God's secrets. (In our work, as in any business, one of the chief requirements of a trustee is honesty.) It doesn't make any difference to me whether I'm sized up by you or some other personnel committee; in fact, I can't even size up myself! I know next to nothing about myself, but that doesn't excuse me. The one who finally passes on me is the Lord himself. So don't jump to conclusions ahead of time. For the Lord himself comes and illuminates the dark secrets and makes clear the intent of our hearts. At that time God will give each man his proper credit.

6. Now brothers, I've applied all this to myself and Oliver so as to help you see in us that one should not go beyond what has been spelled out, and that one should not vie with another in puffing himself up. After all, who put *you* on a pedestal? What have you got that was not *given* to you? Well then, if it's a *gift*, why do you brag as though you *earned* it? Yeah, you're rich all right. You've piled it sky-high. You can even rule the roost without any help from us. Indeed! How I wish that you did rule, so we could share your throne!

9. You know, I think God has made us preachers the bottom men on the totem pole, like men on death row, because we've become a morbid curiosity to the men and women of the world. For Christ's sake *we* are fools, but you, *you* are doctors of divinity. We are the nobodies, while you belong to the establishment. You are the elite, while we're scum. Even at this very moment we're hungry and thirsty and ragged. We get our heads cracked, we're shoved and pushed around, and work like dogs to make a living with our own hands. Though cussed out, we bless. Though persecuted, we restrain ourselves. Though lied about, we reply gently. We have become like a garbage dump for the world, being right now a place for everybody's dirty dishwater.

14. I'm not writing like this to make you ashamed of your-selves; I'm doing it to correct you as though you were my own dear children. For even though you may have countless *teachers* in Christ, you don't have many *fathers*. For it was I who sired you in Christ by the gospel. Now I beg you to act like me. This is exactly why I sent to you Timothy, my dear and loyal son in the Lord, that he might refresh your memory concerning the ways I follow Christ, exactly as I teach in every church everywhere. When I did not personally come to you some of you acted smart. All right, the Lord willing, I shall come to you very shortly, and I'll look, not for the talk of the smart fellows, but for their commit-ment. For the God movement is not a way of talking glibly but of living powerfully. So how do you want it? Shall I come to you with my belt, or with a spirit of loving persuasion?

5.

1. It is heard all over that there is sex sin among you, and of a kind that not even non-church-members practice, such as a man sleeping with his stepmother. And instead of going around with your head up in the air, shouldn't you have been concerned enough to remove from your midst one who does such a thing? Though I'm not there physically, I am present in the spirit. Being thus in your midst, I've already decided what should be done about the man doing this thing. All of us (I'll be there in the spirit) should get together in the name of the Lord Jesus, and acting under the au-thority of our Lord Jesus, we should surrender this person to Satan to finish wrecking his appetite so that his soul might be saved on the day of the Lord.

6. There's nothing good about your bragging. Don't you know that even a few germs will contaminate the whole dish? Clean up the source of infection, so that you might be a wholesome dish, uncontaminated, just as you are supposed to be. Since the "meat" of our meal—Christ—has already been prepared, let us feast, not on the old contaminated food nor on the germ-laden dish of evil and wickedness, but on the pure food of honesty and truth.

9. I wrote in my other letter to you that you should not mix with tom-catters. I did not mean the tom-tatters, the profiteers, the exploiters and the money-mad who are a part of this world, since you would then have to withdraw entirely from the world. Now what I meant was that if he is *a member of the church* and is a tom-catter or a profiteer or a money addict or a character-assassin or a drunk or an exploiteer, then you should not have fellowship with him. In fact, you shouldn't even eat with him. For what right do I have to judge those outside the church? It's the *church members* you are to discipline, isn't it? God will tend to the outsiders; you clean up the mess in your own ranks.

6.

1. How dare you take your complaints against one another to pagan law courts and not before your fellow believers! Or are you unaware that the believers will eventually try the world? Now if the *world* is to be tried by you, aren't you qualified to hear trivial misdemeanors? And you know, don't you, that we shall sit on cases involving not only affairs of the world but of angels. Then why in the world do you take cases between you, involving mere temporal affairs, before people who have not even been accepted into the church? I say, "Shame on you!" Surely it can't be that you don't have among you a single person wise enough to decide cases among brothers, can it? Yet brother goes to court against brother, and—of all things—before outsiders! Already you've lost stature by having lawsuits at all against one another. Why not rather accept injustice? Why not rather be cheated? But instead, you yourselves practice injustice and fraud, and even worse, on your own brothers! Or maybe you didn't know, huh, that the unjust will have no part in the God movement? Well, don't kid yourselves. No tom-catters, nor money addicts, nor wife-swappers, nor the idle rich, nor homosexuals, nor crooks, nor profiteers, nor drunks, nor char-acter-assassins, nor exploiters will have any part in the God move-ment. Some of you *used* to do these things, but you were cleaned up and given a fresh start; you were made morally sensitive by the name of the Lord Jesus Christ and by the Spirit of our God.

12. All things might be legal for me but not beneficial. All things might be legal, but I don't have to let anything make me addicted to it. One man "lives to eat" and another "eats to live," but God controls the destiny of both. The body is not for tom-catting around, but for the Lord, and the Lord is for the body. It was God's power that raised the Lord and will raise us too. Aren't you aware that your bodies are Christ's limbs? Then shall I take the arms and legs of Christ and make them the arms and legs of a whore? Of course not! Don't you also know that whoever joins up with a whore has one and the same body with her, because it says that "the two shall be the same flesh." It's also true that who-ever joins up with the Lord has one and the same spirit with him. So stay away from whoring. Any other sin that a man commits is against someone else, but whoring is a sin against himself. Don't you know too that your body is a shrine for the indwelling Holy Spirit which you received from God? You don't own yourselves; someone paid dearly for you. Let your body be a credit to him.

7.

1. Now concerning the items in your letter, it is best for a man to stay away from a woman entirely. But because of the prevalence of extramarital intercourse, let each man keep to his own wife, and each woman to her own husband. The husband should com-pletely satisfy his wife, and the wife should do the same for her husband. For the wife is powerless over her own body and must depend on the man to satisfy her. Likewise, the man is powerless over his own body and must depend on the woman to satisfy him. Don't hold yourselves back from one another, unless possibly when both of you have agreed to abstain for a while in order to have more time for prayer. Then come together again, so Satan won't use your abstinence as a means of tempting you. (I'm saying this by the way of permission—not command. For I'd like all men to be single like me; yet each has his own assignment from God, one this, another that.)

8. Let me say this to the unmarried and the widowed: It's best for them to stay single, as I am. But if they can't control their passions, they should get married. For it is better to marry than to be aflame with desire.

10. And for the married I have this command, not from me but from the Lord, that a woman should not separate from her husband (if she does separate, she should either remain unmarried or make up with her husband) and that a man should not leave his wife. Speaking personally, and not for the Lord, I say to the rest of you that if a brother has a wife who is not a Christian, and she is willing to stay with him, he should not divorce her. And if a sister has a husband who is not a Christian, and he is content to live with her, she should not divorce the man.

14. For the non-Christian husband is identified with us through his wife, and the non-Christian woman through her husband. Otherwise, your children would be mixed up, but as it is they too are identified with the movement.

15. However, if the non-Christian wants to separate, let him separate. In such instances the brother or sister is not obligated to stay with the partner, since God has called us to a life of peace. Besides, how do you know, dear lady, but that this will win over your husband? And how can you be sure, sir, but that this might win over your wife?

17. However, each person should accept the situation to which the Lord has assigned him and the responsibility God has laid on him. This is what I instruct all the churches. Were you a white man when you responded to God's call? Don't black your face. Were you a Negro when you were converted? Don't try to be a white man. For the thing that really matters is not that you're white or black, but your obedience to God's commands. Let every man press on as he was when God converted him. Were you a slave when you were converted? Don't be ashamed of it. But just the same, if you can get your freedom, do so. For in the Lord's fellowship a converted slave is the Lord's freedman. By the same token, a converted freedman is Christ's slave. You have been bought and paid for. Don't, then, hire out to men. I repeat, brothers, let each man press on as he was when God converted him.

25. I do not have any specific instructions from the Lord for those who have never married. However, as one who, by the Lord's mercy, is reliable, I venture my personal opinion. I sincerely believe that, due to the present unsettled conditions, it is best for a person to stay as he is. Are you married? Don't seek a divorce. Are you single? Don't try to get a partner. But even if you should marry, you haven't sinned, nor has the girl you marry sinned. It's just that I would spare you all the physical difficulties that those who do get married will have. I'm telling you this, my brothers, we don't have much time left. During what little there is, people who have wives are in the same boat as those who don't, and those who cry are the same as those who smile, those who laugh as those who frown, those who buy are the same as the ones who didn't bid, and they who make room for the world are in the same boat as those who never had any use for it. For the whole structure of the world is collapsing. How I wish you might be free from such worries!

32. The single man's primary concern is for spiritual matters—how he might please the Lord. But the married man's chief worry is how to make a living for his family, and so he is inwardly torn. It's the same with women—the elderly maid and the eligible maiden can devote themselves to spiritual affairs, so as to be dedicated in both body and soul. But the married woman is constantly worrying about her husband and house. I'm saying this not to bridle you but for your own good, so that you can give yourselves without reservation to a well-arranged and determined Christian life.

36. Now if anyone feels that he hasn't done quite right by his marriageable daughter, and if she is already of age (and this she most certainly should be), let her do as she wishes: she isn't sinning; let them marry. However, he who has firmly made up his own mind, being under no pressure but having the right to keep his marriageable daughter, he is doing nothing wrong. So, whoever marries off his daughter does all right, but he who does not marry her off will do better.

39. A wife is bound to her husband as long as he is alive. If he dies, she is free to remarry, but only to a Christian. In my judgment, though—and I think I speak as one who has God's Spirit—she would be far happier if she remained a widow.

8.

1. Now about working on Sunday,[2] we know that we all have been "enlightened." But "enlightenment" is inflating, while *love* makes a man truly great. If someone thinks he knows it all, he hasn't begun to learn the first lesson. Yet if one really loves God, God then opens himself up to him. So back to this working on Sunday, we know that a day means nothing whatsoever, and that God alone really matters. Even though there are also many special days on both Catholic and Protestant calendars, such as those to saints and special events, still for us God alone is supreme, our Father, the source of all things. We are his, and so is the Lord Jesus Christ, through whom are all things, including ourselves. But not everybody has this insight. Some people, because of their tra-

---

[2]The phrase here is literally "eating meat which had been part of a pagan sacrifice," and which was offered for sale in the marketplace. Some had religious scruples against eating it, some didn't. The issue was about parallel to our "working on Sunday."

.ditional background, still think of working on Sunday as sinful, and their sense of right, limited as it is, is offended by it. Well, work of itself doesn't make us .spiritually presentable. So if we don't work we're no worse off, and if we do work, we're no better off. Just be careful that in the exercise of this freedom you do not trip up your weaker brothers. For suppose one of them sees you, an enlightened man, working on Sunday, won't it be too much for his limited understanding and cause him, against his better judgment, to work too? In this way the weaker brother is torn apart by your enlightenment. And since he too is a brother for whom Christ died, when you sin against such brothers and offend their limited understanding, you also sin against Christ. That's why, if working on Sunday spiritually wounds my brother, I'll never work on Sunday as long as I live—but only to keep from spiritually wounding my brother.

9.

1. Who says I'm not "emancipated," that I'm not a qualified preacher? Haven't I seen our Lord Jesus? Aren't you yourselves evidence of my work for Christ? Even though some others don't regard me as an ordained minister, you should, for you all make my Christian ordination authentic. My answer to those who question my integrity in this: Now isn't it true that all of us ministers have the right to bed and board from our congregations? Don't we have the right to have our wife or a sister accompany us, as do the other ministers and the brothers of the Lord and Rock? All right, is it just Barnabas and I who don't have the right to give up making our own living? What soldier ever goes to war at his own expense? What farmer sets out an orchard and doesn't eat of the fruit? In saying this am I guided by human reasoning, or does the Bible itself say the same thing? It says in the Old Testament, "You shall not muzzle a mule while he is plowing corn." Was this said because a mule matters that much to God, or was it entirely for our benefit? It was written for our benefit, of course, because a farmer should be assured of his share of his products, and the hired hand that he has a right to the food he helps produce. If we, then, planted spiritual seeds among you, why the big fuss if we harvest mere material things from you? If others have this right over you, don't we even more? Yet we never did use this right, and we supported ourselves all the way through so as to give no one a chance to bellyache about the gospel of Christ.

13. You know, don't you, that religious workers get their living from donations, and any others connected with the organization share in the contributions. Likewise, the Lord also instructed that they who preach the gospel should get their living from it. But as for myself, I have never made use of any of these privileges. Nor have I written in this vein that it might be so with me now. For I'd much rather die than—no one is going to rob me of that of which I'm so proud.[3] If I merely preach the gospel, that's nothing to brag about, because I'm under compulsion to do that! I'd catch it if I didn't preach the gospel! Now if I do something voluntarily, I get paid for it. But if I'm conscripted, I am bound by superior orders. What then is my "pay"? Being able to preach and establish the gospel free of charge, so as not to exercise in the least my right to sustenance from the gospel.

19. Being thus independent of everyone, I became a slave to everybody in order to reach more people. I related to white people as a white man in order to reach white people; to members of the established church as a church member (though I myself don't belong to one) that I might reach church members; to the uncommitted people I related as an uncommitted man—I was never uncommitted to God but fully committed to Christ—so as to reach uncommitted people. To the powerless people I became a powerless man, to reach people who have no power. In every way I have related to those in all walks of life, if somehow, some way, I might get through to them. Everything I do is for the gospel, that I may be a full partner in it.

---

[3]Paul does not complete this sentence.

24. You don't need to be reminded that while many may compete in a racing event, only one wins first prize, so go all out for top place. Every serious contestant puts himself through rigorous discipline—they to win a tarnishable trophy, but we an enduring life. So I don't want to run like a guy who is unsure of himself or like a boxer flailing the air. Instead, I put my body through terrific workouts and thoroughly master it, because I don't want to preach to others and wind up a dismal failure myself.

10.

1. I don't want you to forget, brothers, that all our ancestors were guided by the cloud, and all of them made it through the sea. (This cloud and sea experience was, in a sense, an initiation into the Moses movement.) They all ate the same miraculous food and they all drank the same miraculous water, for they were drinking from a miraculous, ever-present rock, which was a symbol of Christ. But even so, God wasn't particularly fond of them, for they were discarded in the wilderness. These people became our "lighthouses," to warn us against following their example of hankering for wickedness. Never make a god of your possessions as some of them did. For we are told that "The people sat down to eat and drink the sacrificial meal, and then got right up and started carousing around." Don't go back on God, as some of them did one time when twenty-three thousand came down with disease and died. Let's never try to argue with the Lord, as some of them did and died from snakebite. Never bellyache, like some of them did and were visited by the Death Angel. These things happened to them as sort of a symbol, and were written down for the guidance of us for whom the end of an age has arrived.

12. Let the man who thinks he has his feet on the ground be careful lest he slip and fall. Yet only temptation of a human sort ever overtakes you, and God can be trusted not to let you be tempted beyond your capacities, always providing along with the temptation a way out, so you can be victorious.

14. So then, my loved ones, shun the worship of things with all you've got. I'm talking to intelligent people, so decide for yourselves on what I'm saying. Isn't the blessed cup we reverence a "community" (a *koinonia*) of Christ's blood? Isn't the loaf we break a "community" (a *koinonia*) of Christ's body? Just as the loaf is a whole, so we, though many, are a whole body, for we all took a part of the whole loaf. Take an example from the Jewish ritual: It's true, isn't it, that they who eat the sacrifices are knit together around the altar? So what am I saying? That merely taking part in a ceremony means anything? Or that there's something holy about a ritual? Not at all. I mean simply that worldly people are drawn together in their allegiance to wickedness, not to God. And *I don't want you to be their partners in their evil.* You cannot drink from the Lord's cup and the world's mug at the same time. You can't feel equally welcome at the communion table and at a nightclub. Do we want to get the Lord all riled up? Do you think we can outdo him?

23. Sure, sure, "everything is legal," but that does not mean that everything is beneficial. Sure, "everything is legal," but that doesn't make it right. The best guide is to seek, not your own welfare, but the good of your neighbor. So eat whatever comes from the supermarket—kosher or not—without raising questions of conscience. For after all, everything—the earth and all that's in it —belongs to the Lord. If a non-church-member invites you for a meal, and you wish to accept, go ahead and eat whatever he puts in front of you without raising conscience questions. But if he tells you outright, "This isn't kosher," don't eat it for the sake of your host and his scruples—*his* scruples, I remind you, not your own. And why should *I* let *my* freedom be pushed around by another's scruples? Or if I've said grace, why should I let myself be embarrassed over food for which I've already given thanks? Simply this: Whether you're eating or drinking or whatever, make sure it is to God's credit. Set a good example for both whites and Negroes —for God's whole church—just as I myself favor others in every way possible. I'm not out to have my own way, but to do what's best for others, so they can be saved. Imitate me in this, even as I imitate Christ.

11.

1. Let me commend you for remembering all my lectures and for carrying out the instructions I gave you. Now I don't want you to forget that the head of every man is Christ; that the head of the woman is the man; and that the head of Christ is God. Any man who prays or preaches with his head (Christ) obscured is a shame and a disgrace to his head. On the other hand, a woman who prays or preaches *without* obscuring her head (or husband) is a shame and disgrace to him. It is the same as though she herself were a man. Now if a woman isn't going to act like a lady, then let her get a man's haircut. But if she is ashamed to get clipped and shaved like a man, then she should act like a lady. Indeed, since a man bears the image and honor of God, he should not, like a woman whose "honor" comes through her husband, veil his face. For the man, you know, was not formed from a woman, but the woman from a man. Also, it was the *woman* who was created to be *man's* helper, not vice versa. That's why a woman needs someone to exercise authority over her the same as other "angels." But really, in the Christian fellowship a woman is no different from a man, and a man no different from woman. For even though the woman was formed from the man, it's the woman who gives birth to a man, and God is the creator of both.

13. You all consider this very carefully: Is it proper for a woman to pray to God while vainly exposing her face? Doesn't nature herself teach you that it's a disgrace for a man to let his hair grow, while for a woman long hair is attractive. And besides, it makes a very convenient veil! Now if anybody wants to argue this point, let me simply say that this is standard policy throughout the churches.

17. Now let me lay this on your heart, for I surely don't praise you when your meetings turn out to be not a help but a hindrance. In the first place, I hear that when you assemble as a church you are split this way and that, and I am inclined to believe it. And it's necessary, huh, to have conflicting points of view so that the real truth might come to light? So when you come together it isn't to eat the supper the Lord's way. For each one takes his own private basket to eat from, and some wind up hungry and some stuffed. Couldn't you have stayed at home and eaten like that? Or do you actually have contempt for God's church and embarrass the have-nots among you? What can I possibly say to you? Shall I praise you? I'd never praise you for something like this.

23. Now I myself got it straight from the Lord, and transmitted it to you, that on the night he was turned in, the Lord Jesus took a loaf of bread and after giving thanks he broke it and said, "This is my body, which represents *you all;* make *this* into my memorial." For every time you eat this loaf and share this cup, you clearly declare the Lord's death—until he returns.

27. So then whoever disrespectfully eats the loaf and drinks the cup is actually showing disrespect for the body and blood of the Lord. Let every man carefully examine his own heart, and in the light of this let him eat from the loaf and drink from the cup. For he who eats and drinks without being fully aware of the *body* idea, eats and drinks a sentence on himself. This is why quite a few of you are weak and sickly and some are just plain dead. If we carefully examined our own hearts, we wouldn't come under judgment. But when we are judged by the Lord, we are punished to keep us from being damned along with the world. So then, my brothers when you get together to eat, be considerate of one another. If somebody is so hungry he can't wait, let him eat at home, lest your meeting become a time for judgment. I'll tend to the other matters when I get there.

12.

1. Now brothers, I don't want you to be in the dark on spiritual matters. You are aware that before you were converted your lives were completely dominated by false gods. So I'm making it plain to you that nobody speaking under the influence of God's Spirit ever says, "Jesus be damned." And nobody has the power to say "Jesus is Lord," except through the Holy Spirit.

4. Though there is a difference in what we receive from the Spirit, it is one and the same spirit. Though there are different forms of service, the Master is the same. And though God uses different means of empowering us, it is one and the same God who energizes everybody in every way.

7. To each has been given that aspect of the Spirit which is beneficial to all. To one the Spirit has given a keen mind. To another has been given the capacity for faith, to another a talent for healing, to another the ability to work miracles, to another to preach, to another a sensitive spiritual insight, to another a catalog of tongues and to still another the ability to interpret the tongues—all these prompted by one and the same Spirit, who distributes them to each person as he thinks best.

12. It's just like the body, which is entire within itself, even though it has many parts. With all its parts, it is still only one body. That's the way it is with Christ. For through one Spirit we all—whether whites or Negroes, laborers or white-collar workers —were initiated into one Body, and all of us had one Spirit breathed into us. For the body does not consist of just one part but many. If the foot should say, "Since I'm not a hand, I don't belong to the body," would this make it so? Or if the ear should say, "Since I'm not an eye, I don't belong to the body," would this make it so? If the whole body were an eye, how could it hear? Or if it were an ear, how could it smell? But as it is, God has arranged every single part of the body according to his own design. If everything consisted of just one part, how could it be a body? Now indeed the parts are many but the body is a unit. So then, the eye can't say to the hand, "*I* don't need *you*," nor again, can the head say to the foot, "*I* don't need *you*." But rather, those parts of the body which seem to be most insignificant are extremely important. And those parts of the body which are seemingly the least prized turn out to be quite valuable, and our inconspicuous parts are all the more conspicuous when the conspicuous parts can't meet the same needs. God has delicately balanced the body by giving greater preference to the weaker part so as to avoid discord in the body. In this way the members must exercise the same concern for each other. So if one part suffers, all parts suffer together; if one part gets glory, all the parts share the joy together. Now you all are Christ's body; each one is a part of a larger whole.

28. And God has arranged it in the church that some should be (1) apostles, (2) preachers, (3) teachers, then specialists, then talents for healing, interns, administrators, and a whole slew of talkers. They can't all be apostles, can they? Or preachers? Or teachers, or specialists, or doctors, or talkers in tongues, or interpreters for the tongue-talkers? Yearn for the superior talents. And I want to show you the greatest way of all:

13.

1. Though I speak with the tongues of men and of angels, but have no love, I am a hollow-sounding horn or a nerve-wracking rattle. And though I have the ability to preach, and know all the secrets and all the slogans, and though I have sufficient faith to move a mountain, but have no love, I am nothing. Even though I renounce all my possessions, and give my body as a flaming sacrifice, but have no love, I accomplish exactly nothing. Love is long-suffering and kind. Love is not envious, nor does it strut and brag. It does not act up, nor try to get things for itself. It pitches no tantrums, keeps no books on insults or injuries, sees no fun in wickedness, but rejoices when truth prevails. Love is all-embracing, all-trusting, all-hoping, all-enduring. Love never quits. As for sermons, they shall be silenced; as for oratory, it shall cease; as for knowledge, it will vanish. For our knowledge is immature, and our preaching is immature; but when that which is mature arrives, it supersedes the immature. For example, when I was a child, I was talking like a child, thinking like a child, acting like a child, but when I became an adult, I outgrew my childish ways. So, on the childish level [i.e., *without love*] we look at one another in a trick mirror, but on the adult level [i.e., *with love*] we see face to face; as a child [i.e., *without love*] I understand immaturely, but as an adult [i.e., *with love*] I'll understand just as I'll be understood. Now these three things endure: faith, hope and love; but the greatest of all is love. Seek diligently for love.

14.

1. Yearn for the spiritual gifts, too, especially in your preaching. For when one speaks while in a trance, he is not addressing men but God, and nobody catches on to what he is saying, for by means of a Spirit he is talking about hidden things. But when one *preaches*, he is speaking to men for their encouragement and inspiration and enlightenment. He who speaks in a trance benefits only himself, but he who preaches benefits the whole congregation. I'd like for all of you to be able to speak in a trance, but I'd much rather you'd simply preach. For preaching is much better than speaking in a trance, except perhaps when someone can interpret so the whole congregation might be benefited. Now brothers, suppose I come to you speaking in a trance. Would it do you any good unless what I had to say were in the form of an insight or instruction or a sermon or a lesson? Why, even lifeless things, such as a trombone or a violin, make a sound, but unless it produces clearly discernible notes nobody recognizes the tune. Or if a bugle blows an unrecognizable call, who will know to prepare for battle? Well, that's the way it is with you too. If in a trance you say something unintelligible, how can anyone catch on to what you're saying? You'll just be batting the breeze.

10. There are all kinds of words in the world, and not one of them is without meaning. But if I don't know the content of a word, I'll be a foreigner to the speaker, and the speaker will be a foreigner to me.

12. In the same way, you too, since you are eager for spiritual gifts, should try to build up the church so it will prosper. Therefore, let him who talks in a trance pray that he may be able to explain it. For if I pray in a trance, my spirit no doubt prays, but my mind is a blank. What good is that? So when I pray with my spirit, I'll pray also with my mind; when I sing with my spirit, I'll sing also with my mind. Now suppose you give a prayer with only your spirit, how will an untutored deacon know when to come in with the "Amen" during your thanksgiving if he doesn't know what in the world you're saying? Your prayer of thanks might be quite all right, but nobody else is benefited by it.

18. I thank God that I can outdo any of you in speaking in a trance. But I'd rather speak five intelligent words in church for the instruction of others than a whole dictionary full of words in a trance.

20. Brothers, don't be intellectual runts. Be a harmless baby as far as evil is concerned, but intellectually you should be mature adults. It is written in the Bible, " 'I will speak to this nation through foreigners speaking a different language, but even so it won't pay any attention,' says the Lord." So then the "different language" (trance-talking) has no significance for loyal church members, but for the disobedient. On the other hand, a clear-cut sermon is not so much for the outsiders as for the members.

23. Suppose that when the whole church comes together everybody is talking gibberish, and then some outsiders or others unacquainted with Christianity come in, won't they think you're off your rocker? But if everyone is speaking God's word clearly and to the point when such an outsider or unacquainted person drops in, then he will be deeply moved and convicted by all that's going on; he will speak openly about his inner feelings, and will burst forth in praise to God, shouting, "God is surely among you people!"

26. So what's this all about, brothers? Just this: When you all get together and one has a song, another has a Scripture verse, another an experience or some trance-talk and another has the explanation, then organize it so everybody can be benefited. If anybody starts trance-talking, say two or at the most three, let them take turns while one explains what each says. If there's nobody around to explain it, let him be quiet in church and pray silently between himself and God.

29. Let two or three preachers talk, and the others evaluate it. If a thought strikes a seated minister, let the first one yield the floor. In this way everybody can do a little preaching one at a time, and all will be instructed and encouraged. But do let the preachers try to control themselves, for God is not a God of confusion but of peace.

34. As in all loyal churches, women should stop talking when they get to church. They just plain aren't allowed to do their talking there, but should give their husbands a chance, as the law says. If they want to learn the latest, let them ask their husbands at *home*. For it's a disgrace to have a woman talking in church.

36. Say, did the word of God originate with you all? Or are *you* the only ones in whom it has been established? Listen here, if any guy considers himself a preacher or other religious worker, let him get it straight that what I'm writing to you is a commandment of the Lord himself. If he ignores this, you ignore him.

39. And so, my brothers, when you preach, put all you've got into it. And don't discourage those who talk in a trance. Let everything be done properly and orderly.

15.

1. Now brothers, let me make clear to you the good news which I originally brought to you and which you received, and in which you've taken your stand, and by which you're finding your way out—that is, if you're still holding on to the word as I gave it to you. If you're not, then your "faith" isn't worth a hill of beans.

3. For among the most important things I turned over to you was that which I myself received—that Christ died for our sins, just like the Bible said, and that he was buried, and that on the third day he was raised, again just as the Bible said. As I got it, he was seen by Rock, then by the twelve. Later he was seen by more than five hundred brothers at the same time. (Most of these brothers are still alive, although some of them have since died.) After this he was seen by James, and then by all the apostles. Last of all, like a baby who was born almost too late, I saw him—I, I who am the least of the apostles—I who am not even worthy to be called an apostle because I tormented God's dedicated people. Only by God's grace I am what I now am! And the favor he showed me was not wasted, for I worked harder than all the rest—not I really, but God's goodness that had hold of me.

11. So what difference does it make whether you get it from me or others—this is what we preach and this is what you believed. And if it is clearly taught that Christ was raised from the dead, how is it that now some of you are saying, "There's no such thing as life after death"? Well, if there's no life after death, then Christ himself is still dead! And if Christ is dead, then our message has no meaning, and your faith also has no meaning. On top of this, we turn out to be untruthful witnesses about God, because we solemnly testified that God *did* make Christ alive, which would be impossible if there's no life after death. For if the dead are not made alive, neither has Christ been made alive. And if Christ hasn't been made to live, your faith is a hollow shell and you're still a bunch of sinners. Moreover, all those who died for Christ died for nothing. If our hope in Christ covers only this life, we of all people are the most to be pitied.

20. But now the fact is that Christ *was* made alive. He is the forerunner of those who have passed on. For since death came through a human being, life after death also came through a human being. Just as everybody inherits physical death through Adam, so do all find newness of life in Christ.

23. Each one has his own turn: First is Christ the forerunner, then those who are bound to him in his movement, and then the climax, when he hands over the New Order to the Father-God, at which time all other rule and authority and power will be superseded. For it is necessary for him to continue in power until he has subdued *all* his enemies, the last of which is death. For the Bible says, "He put *everything* under Christ's rule." (But when it says that everything has been put under Christ, it is obvious that this does not include God himself.) So, when everything has been brought under his rule, then the Son himself shall be under the sway of him who put everything in the hands of the Son, in order that God alone might be supreme.

29. Now another thing: If there's no life after death, what about those people who are being consecrated in behalf of their departed loved ones? What's the point of doing such a thing? Indeed, if there's no life after death, why should we also stand in hourly peril of our lives? Brothers, to keep alive our confidence which I have in Christ Jesus our Lord, I live every day on death row. If from a purely human standpoint I fought the police dogs at Birmingham, what good did it do me? If there's no life after death, then let's rev it up, because when it's over we're just dead ducks.

33. Don't make an ass of yourself. Such shoddy thinking destroys decent conduct. Sober up and quit your sinning. I'm ashamed to say it to your face, but some of you have an abysmal ignorance of God!

35. Now someone will ask: "How do the dead live again? What kind of body do they have?" Listen, silly, when you plant something, it won't come up unless it dies. And what you plant is not the new stalk but just a plain seed of, say, wheat or some other plant. Then God gives to it the form that he thinks best, and to each kind of seed its own particular form. Or take flesh—it isn't all the same. Some of it is in human form, some in the form of animals, some of birds and some of fish. Likewise, there are forms, or bodies, for the afterlife as well as forms or bodies for life on the earth, and each form has its own appearance as does the moon and even the stars, for one star differs from another in appearance. And that's the way it is with the afterlife. Something perishable is planted, and it comes up imperishable. Something weak is planted, and it comes up powerful. A vessel of the mind is planted, and a vessel of the spirit comes up. There's a Scripture which says, "The first man Adam became a rational being." The last Adam (Christ) became a life-creating spirit. Note that the spiritual does not precede the rational, but vice versa. The first man sprang from earth, a lump of clay. The second man sprang from the spiritual realm. Just as the descendants of the lump of clay are themselves lumps of clay, so the descendants of the Immortal One are themselves immortal. And as the lump of clay gave form to us, even so shall the Immortal One give form to us.

50. I'm saying simply this, brothers: Skin and bones just aren't able to get into God's realm of spirit, nor can that which is subject to decay take part in that which is immortal. Listen, I'll let you in on a secret: Not all of us will die, but all of us will be changed. It'll happen in a flash, like the batting of an eye, at the last bugle call. For indeed the bugle will blow, and the dead will live again—eternally—and we shall be changed. For this decaying body has to be outfitted with immortality. When this outfitting takes place, then the Bible verse will come true when it says: "Death sure took a licking. Say, Death, what have you won? And Death, what happened to your stinger?" Sin is death's stinger, and sin's power is the law. Thank you, God, for giving us the victory through our Lord Jesus Christ.

58. And so, my much-loved brothers, stand your ground and don't let anybody shove you around. Always keep up the good work for the Lord, for you know that nothing you do for him is ever wasted.

16.

1. Now a few words about that fund for sharing with church members. I'd like for you all to follow the same plan I recommended to the Alabama churches, namely, that each of you, at the first of the week, set aside in a special fund an amount in keeping with your income. Then when I come, there'll be no need for a fund-raising campaign. Upon my arrival, I'll give the proper letters to the committee you've selected to carry your gift to Charleston and send them on their way. If it seems wise that I should go too, we'll go together.

5. I'll get by your way when I pass through Georgia. For I'll be going through Georgia, and will possibly stay a while with you, or even spend the winter with you. Then you might help me on to my next destination. I don't want to' just pay you a pop call, because I'm hoping to spend quite a while with you, the Lord willing. More than likely I'll stay in Birmingham until Thanksgiving, for a great and vital door of opportunity has opened up for me— and a lot of folks are after my hide, too.

10. Should Timothy get by there, see to it that he is relieved of all worries while with you, because he is carrying on the work of the Lord the same as I. Let no one snub him, and when he leaves to come to me, you all give him a warm send-off, for I'm expecting him here with the other brothers.

12. Now about Brother Oliver, I frequently urged him to visit you all with the brothers but he just plain didn't want to right now. But he will come when he feels the time is ripe.

13. Keep your eyes open, hold on to the faith with all you've got, stand up like a man, develop your muscles. Let your every act be an expression of love.

15. You remember, don't you, that the Stephen family were the first converts in Georgia and that they so arranged their lives as to be at the disposal of the church members. Now I want to lay it on your hearts, brothers, to give yourselves over completely to such leaders and to anyone else who takes hold with us and puts in an honest day's work.

17. It sure is good to see Steve, Lucky, and "Big Bam." They sorta make up for your not being here. They're a big boost to both me and you all. Let's give them a big hand.

19. All the congregations in this area send you their warm greetings. Adrian and Prissy, with the fellowship which meets in their home, send special greetings in the Lord. In fact, all the brothers here send you their best wishes. Give everybody a big hug for me.

> With kindest regards,
> *Paul*

P.S. If a man is not sincere in his discipleship, let him be damned. Come on, Lord! May the Lord Jesus' unmerited favor be with you. My love is with you all in Christ Jesus.

The Second Letter to the Atlanta Christians [II CORINTHIANS]

1.

1. From Paul, by God's will an agent of Jesus Christ, and brother Timothy,

To God's fellowship in Atlanta, as well as other Christians throughout the state of Georgia.

Peace and goodwill to you from our Father-God and from our Lord Jesus Christ. And hail to the Father-God of our Lord Jesus Christ—Father of kindness and God of all helpfulness!

4. He surely does stand by us every time we get into trouble, and in the same way that he stands by us he makes it possible for us to stand by others in their trouble. For just as we often get hurt as a result of following Christ, we just as often get help from following Christ. So regardless of whether we get hurt when we lend you a hand and try to pull you through, or whether we are encouraged by your devotion which enables you to endure the same injuries we suffer, our confidence in you is as solid as a rock. We are convinced that even as you are partners in getting hurt, so also in standing by one another.

8. For we don't want you to be uninformed, brothers, about the trouble that happened to us in the South. We were pressed almost beyond our endurance, until we gave up hope of getting through it alive. Indeed, we were singled out to be killed, and our only hope was not in our own efforts, but in God who makes the dead to live. And he *did* deliver us from such a terrible death, and he'll do it again! We're counting on him even yet to get us out of here. But you too must help us with your prayers, so that your faces, along with many others, might light up with gratitude when we're given our freedom.

12. The thing we're proudest of (our conscience bears this out) is that we behaved ourselves before the world, and especially in front of you, with God-like dedication and sincerity, guided not by strategic reasoning but by God's grace. Now I'm not writing to you a lot of stuff you can't even read, much less understand. I do hope you'll fully catch on, just as you have partly understood us. For *we* are *your* talking point just as you are ours in the dawning era of our Lord Jesus.

15. With this assurance, I planned earlier to come to you so you might have the pleasure of a second visit. Then I plan to go on from there into Mississippi and to come by your way again on my way back from Mississippi. You might then want to lend me a hand in getting to Washington.

17. Now once I've made up my mind on something, do I then treat it lightly? Or when I decide on something, do I arrive at it through human reasoning, so as to qualify it with a "maybe so" or a "possibly not"? God knows that when we give you our word it is not both yes and no. God's Son, Jesus Christ, who was preached among you by us—by me and Silas and Timothy—was never both yes and no, but a resounding yes! For God's many promises, made through his Son, are a strong yes. Even the amen is an affirmation by us of God's glory. It is *God* who organized both you and us into a Christian fellowship and gave us the power to endure. He put his stamp of approval on us and poured into our hearts the first install-ment of the Holy Spirit.

23. May God have mercy on my soul if the real reason I didn't come to Atlanta was that I wanted to be easy on you. It's not that we are trying to be bossy on matters of faith; instead, we work side by side with you to make you happy, because you're making a pretty good go of the Christian life.

2.

1. Now I am determined that I'll never again approach you with unpleasant matters. For when I chew you out, who is left to cheer me up—except you, whom I've chewed out! That's exactly the reason I wrote that letter to you, so I wouldn't have to come and be grieved by the very folks who should be making me happy. I lean so heavily on you that I can't be happy at all unless you are. When I wrote to you, I did so out of a greatly troubled and sad heart, and I shed a lot of tears over it. I did it, not just to be raking you over the coals, but that you might understand how much I love you people in particular.

5. Now when a person inflicts injury, he injures not only me but to a certain extent—and I don't want to keep mentioning this—you all too. I looks now as if the punishment decided on by the majority for so-and-so has been adequate, so that from now on you should have a forgiving and encouraging attitude towards him in order to keep him from drowning in his excessive remorse. So I'm urging you to go out of your way to show your love for him. (I've written in this vein partly to see just how obedient you are on all points.) When you forgive somebody for something, I do too. And if indeed I forgave anything—that is, if I had anything to forgive— I did it, for your sake, before the eyes of the Christian body to keep Satan from running over us. For we certainly are on to *his* schemes.

12. Well, when I got to Tennessee with Christ's good news the Lord opened the door wide open for me, but I was worried half sick because I didn't find my brother Titus there. So I told the folks good-bye and hightailed it for Mississippi. (Thank you, God, through whom "we shall overcome"—always—in our commitment

to Christ, and who, through us, wafts the fragrance of knowledge
of him from place to place.) To both those who are being rescued
and those who are perishing we Christians are God's perfume. We
smell like something dead to one, like the breath of life to the
other. Who is capable of such a responsibility? For we are not,
like many others, hucksters of God's word. Rather, when we speak,
it is out of sincerity, as though we are from God and standing before him in Christ.

3.

1. Are we beginning to blow our own horn again? Or do we
need, as some do, to exchange credentials with one another? *You
folks* are our credentials, inscribed on our hearts, easily understood and plainly read by all men. It is clear that you are Christ's
letter being delivered by us, not written with ink but with the
Spirit of the living God; not carved in marble but carved in warm
human hearts.

4. Such dead certainty towards God we get through Christ. We
simply can't make the grade on our own. By ourselves we can't
even get to first base. Our pep comes from God, who also fired us
up to be champions of a new way of life which consists, not of a
lot of talk, but of a new spirit. For words deaden, but the Spirit
gives life.

7. All right, then, if the dead system made up of words typed
on stones was something wonderful to behold (Moses' face was
lit up temporarily so brightly that our forefathers couldn't look at
him), won't the spiritual system be all the more wonderful? For
if the system based on law and punishment was wonderful, won't
the system based on goodness be all the more wonderful? In fact,
that which at one time seemed so wonderfully good now looks
pretty shabby beside something that's so much finer. For if the
temporary was great stuff, the eternal is even more so.

12. Being thus sure of our ground, we come right out into the open. We are not like Moses, who put a mask over his face to keep the Israelites from seeing the end of his fading brightness. Besides, their thinking was in a rut. Why, even to this very day that same mask encrusts the reading of the Bible, and it is torn off *only* by Christ. That's right, up until the present, whenever the Bible is read, a mask lies over peoples' hearts. But whenever a person turns completely to the Lord, the mask is broken off. Now the Lord is spirit, and where the Lord's Spirit rules, so does freedom. And all of us, with our unmasked faces clearly reflecting the Lord's loveliness, are at the same time being changed into his exact image by one glorious thing after another. Thus we take on the Lord's Spirit.

4.

1. So then, since God has shared this responsibility with us, we are not going to chicken out. And what's more, we're making a clean break with shameful secrets and with playing the imposter. Nor are we going to twist the Scriptures. On the contrary, by coming out plainly for the truth we lay ourselves, in God's presence, squarely on the conscience of every man. So even though our good news is unclear, it is unclear only to those whose lives are falling apart at the seams. They have let the god of things blind their faithless minds so that the illumination of the glorious good news of Christ, who is the very image of God, could not penetrate them. It is not ourselves, I tell you, that we're preaching; it is *Jesus Christ as Lord*, for whose sake we are your humble servants. For the God who said, "Let the light shine in darkness," has shined in our hearts so as to floodlight the wonderful knowledge of God beaming in Christ's face.

7. Imagine it! A priceless thing like that in clay pots like us! It just proves all the more that the real power is from God and not from ourselves. Just look! We catch it from every direction but we don't let them squeeze the life out of us. We don't know which end is up, but they don't upend us. We are persecuted, but never wiped out. We are banged all over, but they don't get rid of us. On every hand we bear the *slaying* of Jesus in the body so that the *life* of Jesus in our group might be clearly evident. We who live for Jesus always flirt with death, in order that Jesus' life may be all the more evident in our fragile flesh. So while death is operating in us, life too is in you. Having the same spirit of faithfulness described by the Scripture, which says, "I acted, then I talked," we too act, then we talk. We are sure that He who made the Lord Jesus to live again will also make us alive with Him and stand us all up together. Really, this all happened for you, in order that the kindness which overflows onto so many might swell up as a mighty prayer of thanksgiving and praise to God.

16. And that's why we don't poop out. Even if we do look worn out on the outside, we are constantly refreshed on the inside. After all, it will turn out that our little old troubles will be more than outweighed by our eternal glory. We just don't put any stock in outward things but in inner things. For outward things are perishable, while inner things are eternal.

5.

1. For example, we are sure that if our external framework of God's dwelling is pulled down, we still have a house built by God, a house that's not man-made but spiritual and eternal.[1] We are so hungry to be surrounded by our spiritual environment we can hardly stand it in this present setup. We want to appear *clothed* and not naked. For we who are in the church can hardly bear our heavy responsibilities. We want, oh so much, not to be undressed but dressed, so that our dying may be covered over by his living. This is why God has brought us together and has given us the Spirit as down payment.

8. So then, things are always looking up for us. We realize that when we shut ourselves up in the church we shut ourselves

---

[1]The "dwelling" or "house" here seems to refer to the Christian fellowships and not to the individual body.

out from the Lord.[2] For our way of life is based on faithfulness, not on external appearance. We are absolutely certain that we had rather shut ourselves out of the church and shut ourselves in with the Lord. But anyway, whether shut in or shut out, our sole purpose is to please him. For it is necessary for us all to be laid bare before the bar of Christ, so that each may be rewarded for what he did as a church member, whether good or bad.

11. Being aware, then, of a profound respect for the Lord, we urge men on. We have laid ourselves bare before God and, I hope, before your innermost selves as well. No, we aren't showing off in front of you, but we are trying to give you some valid reason for having confidence in us, so that you can stand up to those who put status above spirituality. For whether we're off our rocker, it is for God; or whether we're sober as a judge, it is for you. For we are hemmed in by Christ's love. We are convinced of this: that One died for us all. In a sense, then, we all died when He died for all, so that we may no longer live for ourselves but for Him who died for us and was made alive. That's why, from here on out, we pay absolutely no attention to a person's outward appearance. It is true that we once knew Christ physically, but now we do so no longer. Therefore, if a man is a Christian he is a brand new creation. The old guy is gone: look, a new man has appeared. This is God's doing all the way through. It is he who, through Christ, bridged the gap between himself and us and who has given us the job of also bridging the gap. God was in Christ, hugging the world to himself. He no longer keeps track of men's sins, and has planted in us his concern for getting together. So now we represent Christ and it is as though God were pleading through us. In Christ's behalf we urge you to open up to God. For our sakes God put a man who was a stranger to sin into a sinful situation so that in him we might know what God's goodness really is.

---

[2]The word translated "church" throughout this passage is the Greek word for "body." There is no way of knowing if the writer is referring to his own body or to the body of Christ. If the latter, "church" may be the correct translation.

6.

1. As your partners we urge you not to take God's goodness toward you for granted. For he says:

> I listened out for you at the right time;
> And on Freedom Day I gave you a helping hand.

Look, "the right time" is *now*; "Freedom Day" is *today*.

3. To keep people from making accusations against our cause, we are mighty careful to give them no openings. Under all circumstances we conduct ourselves as God's helpers, whether it be under much pressure or in hardships or great need or difficulties or beatings or jailings or lynchings or prison sentences or sleepless nights or hungry days. Through it all we stand with sincerity, understanding, forbearance, kindness, a pure spirit, open-faced love, the truthful word and the power of God. We are armed with rightness on both left hand and right, whether we are praised or spit on, whether blessed out or blessed. We are crooks who speak the truth, "babes" who know the score, corpses with a lot of wiggle left, flogged men who just won't die, mourners who are forever gleeful, paupers who enrich everybody, have-nots who have it all.

11. We have no secrets, my Atlanta brothers, and our hearts are wide open. You're not being pressured by us; you're catching it from your own inner feelings. Come on now, give us a break. (You'd think I was talking to children.) You all open up too.

14. Don't get hitched up with non-Christians. For what do order and disorder have in common? Or what partnership is there between light and darkness? Or what agreement can Christ and the Devil have? Or what point of contact is there between an obedient man and a disobedient one? Or how can there be an alliance between God's house and a money house? For *we* are the house of the Living God, just as God himself says:

"I will live with them and walk with them;
And I will be their God, and they will be my nation.
So you all come on out from the midst of them,
And live differently," says the Lord.
"Don't dirty yourselves, and I'll let you come in,
And I will be your Father, and you will be my sons and
daughters," says the Almighty God.

7.

1. Backed up by these promises, my dear ones, let us wash off all physical and spiritual filth. Let's consecrate ourselves reverently to God.

2. Say, make room for us, will you? Not a soul have we hurt, not a soul have we corrupted, not a soul have we beat out of anything. I am not saying this to accuse you, for I've said before that deep down we're in this thing together, to live or die as one. I am quite outspoken toward you, because I have a lot of pride in you. I am filled to the brim with encouragement. Even in all our trouble I'm bubbling over with joy.

5. For even when we came into Mississippi our weary bones got no rest, for there was trouble all around. Outside there were fights, inside there were fears. But God, who boosts the lowly, gave us a boost with the coming of Titus. We were lifted not only by his presence but also by the encouraging news he brought from you. He told us about your deep concern, your hurting, your earnest care for me, till I nearly burst with joy.

8. Even though I upset you with my letter, I'm not sorry I wrote it. To be sure, I was sorry, but now that I see that the letter upset you only for a while, I'm quite happy. For the point is not that you were upset, but that you were upset enough to do something about it. Your disturbed condition made you face up to God, so we didn't do too bad by you after all. For a God-facing disturbance which produces a change of heart is a life-giving experience one never regrets. It is quite different from the strain of the world, which ultimately kills a man.

11. Just look at what all this "divine irritation" did for you. It made you get on the ball and defend yourselves. It made you indignant and scared. It revived your concern, perked you up tremendously and made you straighten things out. You cleared yourselves on every single point!

12. So then, even though I wrote to you as I did, it was not because of the one who did the wrong or because of the one who was wronged, but because I wanted you to be fully aware of the godly concern you all have for us. Now I feel much better about things. And not only are we feeling better, but we are especially happy over Titus' joy. You all surely have put his mind at ease. I guess I did build you up pretty high to him, but I wasn't disappointed in you. Rather, just as everything we said to you was the truth, so our bragging to Titus was the truth. And his heart especially goes out to you when he recalls your obedience, how you accepted him with awe and respect. How glad I am that I can fully count on you!

8.

1. We would like to let you know, brothers, about the God-given kindness which the Mississippi churches have. In the midst of trouble that would try any man's soul, their abounding joy and their desperate poverty overflowed in an outburst of generosity. I know for a fact that they voluntarily gave to the limit of their ability and even beyond. In fact, they were earnestly *begging* us for the privilege of having a part in the relief funds for the church members. It is not at all like we expected, because first they gave *themselves* to the Lord and to us as there by God's will. So we have encouraged Titus to go ahead and finish the fund which he previously began among you. And just as you have more than your share of everything—faith, doctrine, knowledge, eagerness and mutual love—may you also have more than your share in this fund. Really now, I'm not trying to boss you around. I'm just comparing the genuineness of your love with their eagerness. For surely you are aware of the favor of our Lord Jesus Christ, how rich he was and how poor he became for your sakes, so that you, through his poverty, might be rich.

10. Now I venture this suggestion: that you would be better off to go ahead now and finish the thing you set out to do a year ago. Support it as wholeheartedly as when the motion was first passed. For if the support is solid, then whatever one brings is acceptable, because one can't bring what one doesn't have. It would not be fair to make it easy on some and hard on you; rather, there should be an equality. At the present time your abundance will supply their need, just as some day their abundance may supply your need. In this way things will even out. It's just as the Scripture says:

The one who took in much got no more than he needed, and the one who took in little got no less than he needed.

16. I thank God for laying on Titus' heart the same deep concern for you, because he not only accepted the challenge but he voluntarily and with much eagerness checked out for your place. We sent with him the brother whose work in the gospel is highly regarded by all the churches. Not only that, but he was elected by the churches (with our support) to be our companion in the fund we are raising for the glory of the Lord himself. We are taking this precaution to keep someone from leveling a charge against us in regard to this splendid sum we are raising. For we intend to do right not only before the Lord but before men as well.

22. Along with them we sent our brother who, in test after test, we found to be exceptionally diligent. Right now he is chomping at the bit to show you how much confidence he has in you. So then, as far as Titus is concerned, he is my partner and helper in working with you. As for our brothers, they are the churches' missionaries, a credit to the Christian cause. So make no bones about your love for them, and come right out before the churches and show that our bragging to them about you was not vain.

9.

1. There is no need for me to write further about the aid fund for the church members. I am quite aware of your willingness. In fact, I've been bragging on you to the Mississippi Christians, saying, "Those Georgia folks were all ready a year ago." Your getting on with this surely did get a lot of them cranked up! So the reason I'm sending the brothers is to make sure that all our big talk about you in this regard is not a lot of whoopla. You know, I told them that you folks were all prepared. Now just suppose that some from Mississippi should come with me and find you are still messing around, how embarrassing all this talk about you "wonderful people" would be to us, to say nothing of you. Therefore, I considered it urgent to ask the brothers to come on over there and wrap up this promised contribution of yours right away. Then it will all be over with when I get there, and will clearly be a contribution on your part and not an extortion on mine.

6. But remember this: "A stingy sower gathers a stingy harvest and a generous sower gathers a generous harvest." Let each person follow the dictates of his conscience, giving neither with complaint nor under compulsion, for God likes to see a man smile when he gives. Now God is able to shower on you every kind of favor, so that when you have plenty of everything for any occasion you yourselves may shower every sort of kind deed on others. It's like the Scripture says:

> He spread it around and gave to the poor peoples;
> His justice is always a sure thing.

10. Well then he who supplies the farmer with seed will also provide you with bread to eat. What's more, he will multiply what

you plant and increase your harvest of justice. When you are so
blessed in every way, and generously share with everybody, it just
sends a prayer of thanksgiving through our whole being. Because,
you know, this worshipful act of sharing is not only overflowing
to meet the needs of the needy Christians, but is also resulting in
an outburst of thankful praise to God. By the convincing evidence
of this offering you are glorifying God in matching belief in Christ's
gospel with obedience and with generous sharing with them and
others. And they will pray for you, being drawn to you by God's
overwhelming favor in you. Thank God for his gift that's simply
out of this world.

10.

1. Now I'd like to appeal to your sense of Christian dedication
and kindness. (Yes, I'm that Paul guy who is such a lamb when
with you and such a lion when away!) Please don't make it necessary, when I get there, to chew you out as I suppose I'll have to
do to those who think that we are still following worldly patterns.
For even though we live in the world, we do not fight on its level.
Our implements of war are not manufactured by the world but
loaded by God for smashing fortresses. With them we explode
learned discourses and every highfalutin wisecrack against the
true knowledge of God. With them we capture every idea and make
it obey Christ. With them we stand ready to give disobedience a fit
—that is, when you know what *obedience* is all about.

7. Face the facts squarely. If a fellow thinks he's a Christian,
let him take another look at himself, for we are Christians the
same as he. All right, suppose I am a little too haughty with the
authority the Lord gave us for building you up and not for tearing
you to pieces. I'll not let that embarrass me. And I'm not saying
that just to give the effect of scaring you with my letters. Somebody might say, "Yeah, yeah, he sure does write powerfully strong
letters, but he doesn't have the guts to say it to your face!" So, let
such a fellow think this over: *We'll do in your presence exactly*

what we are saying in our absence through our letters! Of course, we are not going to get down in the dirt with those self-appointed guys. For they don't have any better sense than to measure themselves by each other and to compare themselves with one another.

13. Now we will not take over beyond our territory, but will stick to the recognized limits God assigned us—and that includes you in Atlanta. No, we are not overstepping ourselves when we include you, for it was we, you remember, who chanced upon you with the Christian gospel. We definitely do not take over the territory in which others are working. We do hope, however, that as your faith expands it will be possible to extend our circuit even more and to preach the gospel in those regions beyond you without barging in on territory already claimed by others. "Let the man who takes over get his authority from the Lord." For it is not the self-appointed man who gets the job, but the Lord-appointed one.

11.

1. Please go along with me in a little silliness. (Well, you'll have to put up with me anyway!) Listen, I have a God-like concern for you, for it was I who married you to Christ like an innocent young lady to her one and only. But just as the snake tricked Eve with his glib talk, even so I fear that your minds will be sidetracked from single-hearted devotion to Christ. For indeed, when somebody comes around preaching some other Jesus than the one we preached, or when you take on a different spirit which you did not get from us, or a gospel different from the one you received from us, you put up with it without batting an eye! All right, I don't think that I'm one inch behind those big-shot preachers. I might be a boring speaker, but there's nothing wrong with my facts. In every way we've made this clear to you time and again.

7. Tell me, did I do wrong by living humbly so that you all could be better off while I preached God's gospel to you free of charge? Why, I even accepted money from other churches, taking pay from them for helping you. And if I got broke while I was staying with you, I didn't go around bumming on anybody—the brothers who came from Mississippi paid my bills. In no way did I allow myself to be a stone around your neck and I'm going to keep it that way. Here's the gospel truth as straight as I can give it to you: this apostolic commission of mine will not be limited to the state of Georgia. How come? Because I don't love you? God knows.

12. Now I shall continue my present course of action, so as to cut off the incentive of those seeking an opportunity to get a commission just like ours. For those fellows are phony preachers, slick operators, who have worked themselves over into Christian ministers. And no wonder, for the Devil too works himself over into a lit-up angel. It's no big surprise, then, when his servants transform themselves into servants of righteousness. One of these days they'll get what is coming to them.

16. Again I say, don't let anybody get it into his head that I'm a crackpot. If so, then just let me go on being a crackpot so I can bring out a few of my own qualifications. (What I'm now saying on this subject of qualification is not to be understood as from the Lord but as something of a joke.) Since many are presenting their external qualifications, I will present mine too. Since you are such wits, you gladly put up with nitwits. You take it even when somebody enslaves you, or when one eats you out of house and home, or when one takes you for a ride, or when one double-crosses you, or when one socks you on the jaw! It's a crying shame, isn't it, that we have been too weak to treat you like that! But, in whatever way another acts big, I'll act big too. (Remember, I'm just kidding.) They are *Americans*—like me. They are *Anglo-Saxons*—like me. They are white men—like me. They are Christians—I'm talking like I'm nuts—I have it all over them. Here's my score:

Days on the work gang—lost count
Number times in jail—lost count

Number times beaten up—too many
Faced with death—quite often
The usual mauling by the State Patrol—five times
Beat with blackjack—three times
Shot—once
Car wrecks—three
Day and night in the swamp—once

The above does not include the number of times I've been on the road or received threats of fire hoses, threats from hoodlums, threats from my own race and from Negroes as well, threats in the city, threats in the country, threats while traveling, threats from phony church members. Many times so dog-tired and worn out I couldn't sleep, hungry and thirsty, frequently postponing my meals, cold and ragged. And on top of this, the anxious concern for all the churches weighed down upon me every day. Who gets sick and I don't get sick? Who gets into trouble and I'm not scorched by it?

30. If it is necessary to be qualified, I'll let my weaknesses qualify me. The God and Father of our Lord Jesus, who is forever blessed, knows that I am not lying.

32. (Add to above list: In Savannah some Klansmen hatched a plot to lynch me, but I was let down in a basket from a fourth-floor window and got away from them.)

12.

1. It's necessary to be qualified, but that alone is not enough. Now I shall come to the subject of visions and the Lord's revealings. Fourteen years ago I knew a Christian man (whether he is still alive or not I do not know—God knows) who was carried away to the third spiritual realm. And I knew a certain fellow—whether he's alive or not I don't know—God himself knows—who was carried away into paradise and heard code words which mortals aren't allowed to repeat. Now I shall present the qualifications of a man like that but not my own, unless, of course, it's my weaknesses. For if I want to exhibit qualifications, I will assure you that I'll be nobody's fool. But I'm foregoing it, so that no one will give me credit for exceptional insight even beyond what one sees and hears of me. Besides, to keep me humble, I was given "a thorn in the flesh"—a real satanic reminder—to harass me and keep me on my knees. When I had spoken to the Lord three times about this and begged him to remove it, he said, "My kindness will see you through it; for strength is achieved in a handicap." Most gladly, then, will I qualify myself all the more with my handicaps, in order that Christ's strength might hover over me. Therefore, for Christ's sake, I gladly accept handicaps, insults, arrests, houndings and tough times. For my strength is rooted in my weakness.

11. I'm talking like a fool, but you shoved me into it. Look, *I* ought to be recommended by *you*. Even though I'm a nobody, I am every whit as good as those big-shot preachers. The marks of the minister were wrought out before you with complete dedication— by miracles, wonders and powerful deeds. Tell me, what is it that makes you feel more neglected than the rest of the churches? Is it that I didn't let you pay me a salary? Please forgive me for hurting you like that!

14. Now look, for the third time I'm getting ready to come to you, and I positively will *not* accept a salary. For I have my eye, not on your wallet, but on *you*. Children shouldn't have to earn a living for their parents; rather, parents should provide a living for their children. Indeed, for your welfare I'd gladly spend my last dime and have the gold picked from my teeth. Should I be loved any less just because I love you so much? All right, so I didn't impose on you, but being a smart cookie I took you for a ride by some clever trick! Well how about that! Did I milk you by any one of those I sent to you? I urged Titus to come to you, and I sent with him our brother. Did Titus milk you? Do not he and I have the same attitude? Don't we wear the same shoes?

19. You're thinking all along that I'm pleading my case before you. Well, I'm not. I'm addressing God through Christ. However, my dear ones, it is all for your spiritual benefit. For I very much fear that when we get together we aren't going to be too pleased with one another. I wonder if there'll be evidence of quarreling, jealousy, hard feelings, taking sides, catty remarks, talking behind another's back, running off at the mouth and general hell-raising. The next time I come, God might bring me low in front of you all, and I'll shed a lot of tears over many of those who have sinned and have never turned away from the filth, the whoring, and the disgusting things they've done.

13.

1. As I said, this will make my third visit with you. "All evidence must be supported by the word of at least two or three witnesses." I said it before when I was with you the second time, and I say it again now that I'm absent from you, that when I get there this time I'll not hold back the works from those who have lived so wickedly, and from all the others too. Since you asked for some proof of the Christ who speaks through me, you'll find that he's no sissy around you, but is dynamite within you. True, he didn't put up a fight when they lynched him, but now he is loaded with God's power. So it is, we too share in his "weakness," but with him *we too are loaded with God's power* in our relations with you.

5. Check up on yourselves to see if you are still Christians. Take an inventory on yourselves. Are you yourselves convinced that Christ is in you, that maybe you *are* bankrupt? Now I hope that it's clear to you that *we* are not bankrupt. We fervently pray not to harm you in any way, not just that we might establish our own solvency but that you might do what's right. Who cares if we *are* called bankrupts! After all, you can't hold the truth down; you can only uphold it.

9. We rejoice when we are scum; but you, when you are the power structure. We sincerely wish for your correction on this point. That's why, though absent, I'm writing these things. Let's hope that when I get there I may not find it necessary to use too sharply the authority which the Lord gave me for building up the church rather than tearing it to pieces.

11. In closing, brothers, I send you my greetings. Correct yourselves, encourage one another, think together, wage peace. And the God of love and peace will be with you. Extend to one another the hand of Christian fellowship. All the Christians here send their regards.

13. The unmerited favor of the Lord Jesus Christ and the love of God and the Holy Spirit's community be with you all.

Sincerely,
Paul

The Letter to the Churches of the Georgia Convention

[GALATIANS]

1.

1. From Paul, a delegate, not from any human organization nor appointed by any human being, but by Jesus himself and by the Father-God who raised him from the dead, and from all the brothers here with me;

To the churches of the Georgia Convention.

3. Warm greetings to you and peace from our Father-God and from the Lord Jesus Christ, who willingly got into our sinful mess with us so as to pull us out of this present-day wickedness. Such was the eternal intent of our Father-God, to whom the credit is due through all ages.

6. I am shocked that you are switching over so soon from the gospel of the one who converted you to Christ's grace to some other "gospel," which really isn't a gospel at all. It is the invention of some fellows who are getting you all confused by trying to rearrange the Christian message. Now get this straight: Even if we or an angel fresh out of heaven preaches to you any other message than the one we preached to you—to hell with him![1] It's just as I told you before and am telling you again now, if anybody brings you a gospel different from the one you received, to hell with him.[1]

---

[1]The Greek is even stronger!

10. All right now, is it God or man that I'm responsible to? Do you think I'm trying to be popular? Well, if I am, then I'm not a committed Christian. I want to make it perfectly clear, brothers, that the gospel message which I preached to you is not of human origin. Neither did I get it from a human being, nor was I taught it. It was opened up to me by Jesus Christ himself. For you are aware of my previous life as a white Southerner, how fanatically I harassed the movement and violently attacked it, and how I went far beyond most white Southerners of my age in zealously defending and promoting the traditions of our noble ancestors. But when He, who changed my course before I was ever born, and by His grace called me—when He spread his good news among Negroes, I did not at first breathe a word of this to any living soul, nor did I go up to Atlanta to talk with the denominational leaders. Instead I went up North, and later returned to Savannah. Then after about three years I did go to Atlanta to visit Rock,[2] and I stayed with him for fifteen days. But I didn't see any of the other leaders except Jim, the Lord's brother. (Honest to God, I'm not lying about what I'm writing you.) From there I went into the mountains of Tennessee and North Carolina. But I was not known personally to any of the Christian groups in Georgia, except that they were hearing that "he who once harassed us is now advocating the way of life he previously attacked." And they were praising God for what he had done in me.

2.

1. Fourteen years later, because of an insight I had, I went again to Atlanta with Barney, taking Titus along with us. There I laid before them the message which I preach among Negroes. (I did this privately before the executive committee, so that what I was

---

[2] The Greek word, Πέτρος, "Peter," means "rock," and is here so translated. His last name was Bar-jonah, which means "son of John" or "John's son" or "Johnson." Thus Peter's full name may be accurately translated, "Rock Johnson."

doing—or had done—might not be wasted.) But not even Titus, the Negro professor who was with me, was compelled to abide by Southern traditions. However, there were some sneaky phony-Christians who slipped in to spy on the freedom which we enjoy in Christ Jesus, so as to make us slaves of their system. But we did not give in to them for one minute, so that the truth of the gospel might be firmly established for you today. But from those on the executive committee (actually I don't care *who* they are; God doesn't recognize human distinctions)—but as I say, those on the executive committee had no changes to suggest to me. Rather, they clearly grasped that I had been made responsible for getting the word to Negroes, just as Rock had been to whites. For obviously the same one who had empowered Rock to work among whites had also empowered me among Negroes. So when they understood the privilege with which God had favored me, Jim and Rock and Jack, the key leaders, warmly shook hands with Barney and me, so that we might work alongside the Negroes, and they with the whites. Their only suggestion was that we always bear in mind the poor, and this I have been most diligent to do.

11. But in spite of all this, when Rock came to Albany I had to rebuke him to his face, because he was clearly in error. For, before the committee appointed by Jim arrived, he was eating with Negroes. But when they came, he shrank back and segregated himself because he was afraid of the whites. He even got the rest of the white liberals to play the hypocrite with him, so that even Barney was carried away by their hypocrisy. But when I saw that they were not planting their feet firmly in the truth of the gospel, I said to Rock right in front of everybody:

If you, a white man, have freely accepted integration and not segregation, how do you now compel Negroes to accept white customs? Here we are, white people by birth and not "inferior niggers." And yet we know that a man can't get right with God just by walking in our Southern way of life. It is only as we *live the way of Christ Jesus*. Now all of us have put our faith in Christ Jesus, so as to be made right by our Christian faith and not by our Southern traditions, because custom never made a saint out of anyone. Now if, in our struggle to be true to Christ, we ourselves wind up segregated, does this make Christ a party to segregation? Heavens no! But if I try to rebuild a wicked system which I've already knocked down, then I may consider myself a violator. For so far as the Southern way is concerned I died, so I could be alive toward God. I was strung up with Christ. I'm no longer alive. It is Christ who lives in me. This physical life which I now have, it is simply an expression of my faith in God's Son who loved me and gave himself for me. I dare not reject God's unmerited favor. For if getting right with God is a matter of observing traditions, *then Christ had no business dying.*

3.

1. You slow-thinking Georgians, who hoodwinked you—you before whose eyes Jesus was graphically portrayed as strung up? I want to learn this from you: Were you converted by keeping the customs or by obeying the faith? Are you all that dumb? Having started out on a spiritual level, are you now winding up on a physical one? Did you suffer so much for nothing—as it may turn out? Does God nourish you on the Spirit and do great things among you when you are keeping the traditions or when you are obedient to the faith?

6. Just as Abraham[3] lived by the Unseen, which was the thing that put him right with God, so you should realize that only those who likewise put their complete trust in God are true "white" men. The Scripture foresaw that God would accept all races on the basis of their faithfulness to him and long ago told the good news to Abraham that "through you *all* races will be given dig-

---

[3]Since Abraham was the father of the Hebrew nation, or the first Jew, we would need to think of him, in the Southern context, as "the first white man."

nity." So then, all of those who share Abraham's *faithfulness* are accorded his *dignity*.

10. People who try to observe the taboos and customs are really in a bad way, for society says, "Woe to that man who doesn't abide by *everything* prescribed by our Southern heritage and way of life." Yet it is as clear as day that nobody ever got right with God by the traditions, because "God's man shall stand on his faithfulness." But customs are not based on faithfulness to God but on a strict adherence to the customs themselves. Christ liberated us from the damning effects of the customs by letting them fall on him instead of on us, just as they say, "Whoever gets strung up on a tree is a damned fool." The inner purpose of his doing this was that Negroes might be accorded the dignity of white men in the Christian fellowship, and that we all, by our faithfulness, might receive the assured support of the Spirit.

15. Brothers, let me give you a human example. Nobody is free to disregard or change a man's contract once it has been signed and recorded. Now God's contract stated that it was with "Abraham and his child." It does not say, "and with his children," plural, but "child," singular. Now this "child" is Christ. So this is what I'm saying: Our customs, which arose several hundred years later, do not supersede the contract previously entered into by God nor nullify its agreements. For if our heritage springs from our social customs, then it is no longer bestowed by God. Yet in the case of Abraham (our illustrious forefather), the privileges were freely bestowed by God, not tradition.

19. Well then, what about our Southern way of life? It was intended to keep down friction until "the child" mentioned in the contract should come and, like a mediator, set things right with the help of his assistants. However, a mediator never represents just one party, even though God himself is one of the parties. Is the Southern way, then, contrary to God's principles? Not necessarily. For if the South's traditions can lift a man to a more noble life, then surely something good and right has come from it. But the trouble is that the Scripture has labeled it all under the heading of sin, so that the assurance of the Christian faith might be given to those who *live* by it. Before the coming of the faith, we were walled in by tradition, hemmed in, awaiting the approaching faith that was to be unveiled. So in a way, the Southern customs disciplined us for the Christian life, that we might be put right by faithfulness. But now that the faith has come, we no longer need the disciplinarian. For *all* of you are sons of God by virtue of the Christian faith. You who were initiated into the Christian fellowship are Christian allies. No more is one a white man and another a Negro; no more is one a slave and the other a free man; no longer is one a male and the other a female. For you *all* are as *one* in Christ Jesus. And if you are Christ's men, then you are true "white men," noble heirs of a *spiritual* heritage.

4.

1. Now let me say this: All the while an heir is a minor, even though he is the legal owner of the whole estate, he is really no different from an employee because he is under guardians and administrators until the appointed time set by his father. So it is with us Christians. When we were minors we were ruled by the deeply entrenched patterns of the culture. But when the time for our manhood came, God sent forth his Son—through a woman and into the Southern system—in order that he might rescue those caught by the system and that we might receive our full sonship. Because you are now sons, God has implanted the spirit of his Son in our hearts, and we murmur, "Father, Father." So, you aren't a slave anymore. You are a son. And if you are a son, you are, through God, a noble heir of the heritage.

8. Earlier, when you had no understanding of God, your lives were dominated by the things which, by their very nature, were not "gods" at all. Now, however, since you know God, or rather, since he knows you, how is it that you are turning again to the sick and impoverished patterns which you are bent on kowtowing to? You're going right along with the same old "for whites only" stuff. I'm really concerned about you. I might have wasted my time on you.

12. Be like me, because I'm the same as you. Brothers, I'm pleading with you. You've never been mean to me. You remember that it was because of an illness that I first shared the good news with you and even though physically I was a trial to you, you didn't let me down or run me off. Instead, you treated me like an angel from God, like Christ Jesus. So where's that graciousness of yours? For I'm telling you a fact, if need be you'd have picked out your eyes and given them to me. Surely you don't think I've become your enemy now just because I'm speaking frankly to you, do you?

17. Now listen, those fellows who are giving you the rush are not on the level. They are trying to capture you so you can rush around for them. Now it's all right to make over somebody once in a while, provided it is done sincerely. I do it occasionally when I am not in the presence of you, my children, over whom I agonize again and again until Christ takes shape in you. I surely do wish I could be with you right now and change my tone of voice, because you've got me all befuddled.

21. Tell me something, you who want to be bound by the traditions: Why aren't you *obeying* the traditions? For history tells us that the founder of the white race, Abraham, had two sons—one from a slave woman of his and another from his legal wife. Now the son from the slave women was sired out of plain sexual desire, but the one from the free woman (his wife) was sired through God's intervention. All of which is sort of an allegory, or story. The two women represent two different sources of tradition. One is rooted in slavery, as represented by the slave woman, Hagar. Now Hagar is the slave South, and corresponds to the present-day segregated structure, for her descendants are still pretty much in slavery. But the God-fearing South is *free,* and *she* is our mother. For history sings:

> Paint the town, you childless lady:
> Dance a jig and shout aloud, you wife who had no baby.
> For the children of the barren woman
> Will outnumber hers who has the husband.

28. So we, brothers, like Isaac (the son of the free woman), are the children of God's intervention. But even today it is still very much like it was back there when the boy who was sired in lust persecuted the one who was the product of God's spirit. So what did God say? "Get rid of the slave woman and her boy. The son of slavery shall not be an heir along with the son of freedom." And that's why, my brothers, *we* are not children of a *slave* system, but of a *free* society.

5.

1. It was for this freedom that Christ emancipated us. So stand your ground, and don't let anybody saddle you with that slave system again. Look here, I, Paul himself, am telling you that if you accept segregation,[4] Christ isn't worth a cent to you. Again I solemnly warn every man who accepts segregation that he is duty-bound to abide by the *whole* code. You who look to the Southern way to save you have severed relations with Christ; you have stumbled away from the idea of *unmerited* favor. For *we* are staking our hope of being right with God on a spirit of faithfulness. Because in Christ Jesus neither segregation nor integration[5] is a determining factor; rather, it is faithfulness activated by love.

---

[4]The Greek word actually means "circumcision," which was the initiatory rite into Judaism. Since it was the symbol of being a Jew, or in our context, a white man, it would mean to the ancient Jew about the same thing as our word, "white Southerner." Thus "a circumcised Jew" would be the near equivalent of "a white Southerner," or perhaps more accurately, "a white church member."

[5]The word here is "uncircumcision," used to refer to those who had abandoned the Jewish traditions, or who had never observed them in the first place. They were the nonconformers.

7. You were doing nicely; who drove a wedge between you and the truth? Such doing was certainly not with the consent of him who converted you. Remember: "One rotten apple spoils the whole barrel." I surely hope to the Lord that you won't listen to anybody else. That guy who is stirring you up will have a lot to answer for in the judgment, no matter *who* he is! But in my case, brothers, if I'm still preaching segregation, then why am I still persecuted? Christ's lynching would then offend no one. I wish to goodness that those who are unsettling you were themselves tarred and feathered.

13. So you my brothers, were invited to sit at the freedom table. But even so, don't use your freedom for any physical advantage. Instead, serve one another in a spirit of love. For the whole social code can be summed up in one sentence: Love your neighbor as yourself. But if you snap and bite one another, be careful that you don't eat each other up.

16. My advice is: Walk in the Spirit, and don't let human desire go to seed. For the body has it in for the conscience, and the conscience has it in for the body, for the two are directly opposed to each other. That is why you cannot run wild, doing as you please. Now if you are guided by the conscience, you are not under the sway of social custom.

19. It is clear that the results of being guided by the body are loose sex relations, filthiness, unbridled lust, worshiping gadgets, trickery, hostile feeling, division, jealousy, temper tantrums, boot-licking, snobbery, arguments, envy, tippling, horsing around and things like these. I am calling to your attention now, just as I did previously, that all who practice such things as these will not be counted in on the God movement.

22. On the other hand, the results of the Spirit-led life are love, joy, peace, patience, kindness, goodness, loyalty, humility and self-control. There is no law against things of this nature. And true Christians have subdued the body with its unruly passions and cravings. If we are people of conscience, then let's stick by our conscience. Just don't be arrogant, nor ridicule one another, nor be envious of each other.

6.

1. Brothers, even if a man gets caught at some misdeed, you who are spiritual-minded should straighten him out. But do so with a gentle spirit, always wondering if someday you might not be tempted to do the same thing. For the essence of the Christian life is to shoulder the loads of one another.

3. Now if somebody thinks he is a big shot when he is nothing but a nubbin, he is kidding himself. Each man should size up himself by his own accomplishments, and then he will have pride in himself and not just in what someone else has done. For every man has to stand on his own two feet. Let the student share his material goods with his teacher.

7. Don't let anybody pull the wool over your eyes—you can't turn up your nose at God! For a man harvests exactly what he plants. If he plants the seed of materialism, he will reap the rottenness of materialism. And if he plants the seed of spirituality, he will harvest the superb life which the Spirit produces. So let's not give up the good fight, for our harvest will come in its own good time if we keep on keeping on. Every chance we have, let's work for the good of all, and especially for the members of the church.

11. Look at the size of the following letters which I have written to you in my own hand: THEY WHO FORCE SEGREGATION ON YOU ARE SEEKING THE APPROVAL OF SOCIETY SO THEY WON'T GET PERSECUTED FOR ACCEPTING CHRIST'S LYNCHING. For even the segregationists themselves do not keep the code, but they try to force it on you so they can brag about it. But as for me, God forbid that I should ever take pride in anything, except in the lynching of our Lord Jesus Christ. Through it I have hanged the world and the world has hanged me. So now neither segregation nor integration makes the difference—it's the new man. Let peace and mercy abide on all who hold to this position, on God's true "white people."

17. Finally, let no one have it in for me personally, for on my body I bear the brand marks of Jesus.

18. May the unmerited favor of our Lord Jesus Christ be with the spirit of each of you, my brothers.

Yours,
Paul

The Letter to the Christians in Birmingham [EPHESIANS]

1.

1. From Paul, Jesus Christ's preacher by the will of God;
To all who live a different life because of their faith in Jesus
Christ.
I greet you all and wish you grace and peace from our Father-
God and from our Lord, Jesus Christ.

3. Three cheers for our Lord Jesus Christ's Father-God, who
through Christ has cheered us along the heavenly way with every
possible spiritual encouragement! It was he, you know, who picked
us out before the world began to stand before him as a people apart
and pure. In love he chose us to be his family through Jesus Christ.
This was his gracious will, and it reflects his marvelous kindness
which he has freely given us through his dear One. For it was by
this One's supreme sacrifice that we got our "emancipation," the
forgiveness for the mess we made of things. This act was an expression of his overflowing goodwill which he lavished upon us
with wisdom and insight.

9. Now he has let us in on the secret of his plan, which is to
make Christ head over everything, both spiritual and material.
He'll do this in his own good time, when he thinks things are right.
And it has already been determined at "headquarters," from which
come all directives that get things moving, that we who have put

our trust in Christ shall take part in this plan and be a credit to the cause.

13. You all, too, when you listened to the message of the truth, the good news of a "new way of walking," and put it into action, then the promised Holy Spirit put his OK on you. This is our "certificate of membership," entitling us to engage in the liberation movement set up for God's glory.

15. This is why, when I heard about your Christian living and the love you show towards everybody in the fellowship, I couldn't stop thanking God for you all every time I prayed. And I asked the God of our Lord Jesus Christ, our glorious Father, to give you spiritual wisdom and a better understanding of him. May he give clear sight to your soul's eyes. May you know the hope which his call inspires and the wonderful resources available to Christians because of their membership in his family. May you experience the incredible outburst of his power in us who rely on his might and his abundant energy. This same energy working in Christ raised him from the dead and gave him spiritual victory and authority over every ruler and every governor and every judge and every sheriff and every other title you can name both now and in the future. Furthermore, it brought everything and everybody under his rule, and made him the head of everything in the fellowship, which is his body, the full expression of him who gives meaning to everything everywhere.

2.

1. In days gone by you all were living in your sin and filth like a bunch of stinking corpses, giving your allegiance to material things and ruled by the power of custom. You can still see this spirit working now in the lives of those who won't listen. In fact, at one time or another all of us were following our selfish inclinations and doing just as we pretty well pleased, because we were naturally just as big scoundrels as everybody else. But even though we were a bunch of corpses rotting in our mess, God in his over-flowing sympathy and great love breathed the same new life into us as into Christ. (You have been rescued, I remind you, by divine intervention.) With Christ Jesus he resurrected us and elevated us to the spiritual household. This clearly demonstrates forever the untold richness of his favor which he so kindly bestowed upon us in Christ Jesus. So again I remind you, you have been rescued by his kind action alone, channeled through your faith. You didn't get this on your own; it was God's free gift. So nobody can brag that he himself achieved it. For we are his doing, made for the good deeds which God intended all along for us as Christians to practice.

11. So then, always remember that previously you Negroes,[1] who sometimes are even called "niggers" by thoughtless white church members, were at one time outside the Christian fellowship, denied your rights as fellow believers, and treated as though the gospel didn't apply to you, hopeless and God-forsaken in the eyes of the world. Now, however, because of Christ's supreme sacrifice, you who once were so segregated are warmly welcomed into the Christian fellowship.

14. He himself is our peace. It was he who integrated us and abolished the segregation patterns which caused so much hostility.

---

[1]The Greek word which is commonly translated "Gentiles" has two meanings: (1) From the standpoint of the Jew it refers to all non-Jews, just as the Greeks referred to all non-Greeks as "barbarians." From the standpoint of the white man, "Gentiles" would mean all nonwhites, or specifically in the Southern context, Negroes. It should also be said that from the point of view of colored people, all noncoloreds are "Gentiles." (2) It refers not only to the nondescendants of Abraham according to the flesh, but particularly to those who walk not in his ways. In this respect it would be about the equivalent of non-church-member, or non-Christian.

So, when the racial aspect of the word seems uppermost we have translated it "Negroes," assuming the viewpoint of the "superior" white man of today to correspond to that to the "proud" Hebrew of New Testament times. When the spiritual and ethical meaning is paramount, we translate it with phrases like "the rest of society" or "the people of the world." (4:17)

He allowed no silly traditions and customs in his fellowship, so that in it he might integrate the two into one new body. In this way he healed the hurt, and by his sacrifice on the cross he joined together both sides into one body for God. In it the hostility no longer exists.

17. When he came, he preached the same message of peace to those on both the inside and outside. In him we both found a common spiritual approach to the Father. So then, you are no longer segregated and pushed around, but you are fellow citizens with all Christians and respected members of God's family. This is based on the unshakable foundation Jesus himself laid down through the apostles and other men of God, with Christ being the cornerstone. Around him all the rest of the building is fitted together into a dedicated temple of the Lord. And you all are a vital part of God's spiritual dwelling place.

3.

1. It is for this reason—my own Christian convictions on race—that I, Paul, am now in jail. (I suppose you heard about my assignment on your behalf which, by God's grace, was given to me.) The secret was made known to me by a revelation, about which I briefly wrote before. If you will reread it, you'll clearly understand my insight into this secret of Christ's. You'll also find that it was not made known to the people of former times as now it has been made crystal clear to his dedicated preachers and deeply spiritual men of God.

6. The secret is that the Negroes are fellow partners and equal members, co-sharers in the privileges of the gospel of Jesus Christ. As a result of God's kindness, so freely bestowed on me and so undeserved, I am now an ardent advocate of that gospel. I just can't get over it, that I, the least likely of all the Christians, was chosen for this honor—the honor of explaining to the Negroes the untapped resources of Christ, and to make clear to them what their part is in this insight that God created everybody alike, but which has been so little understood in the past. Today, however, God's richly colored wisdom has been gotten over to the authorities and the leaders in high places by the action of the church. This is in accordance with his eternal intent which he expressed in Christ Jesus our Lord. In him we have the boldness and the confidence to give such an expression to our faith. That's why I beg you not to let the things I'm suffering for you get you down in the dumps. It's for your ultimate benefit.

14. When I think of all this I get down on my knees before the Father who has stamped his image on every race in heaven and on earth, and I beg him to give you, out of his glorious abundance, the power to win by his Spirit ruling your inner life. God grant that Christ, through your faith, might establish residence in your hearts. May love be your tap root and foundation. May you have the strength to grasp with all God's people the width and length and height and depth of the love of Christ which surpasses all human understanding. Let God's fullness fill you.

20. Now to him who is able, by the power energizing us, to exceed all our fondest hopes and aspirations, be the honor in the church and in Christ Jesus, not only for this generation but for all time to come. Please may it be so.

4.

1. As a prisoner in the Lord's cause, I urge you all to walk in a way becoming to the calling with which you were called. Be humble-minded and gentle and patient. Bear with one another in love, and be careful to preserve the spiritual unity within the framework of peace. "One body, one spirit," is the principle on which you all have been called together into one active fellowship. "One Leader, one plan of action, one initiation, one Father-God of all, who is over all and in all."

7. Each one of us received a measure of Christ's favor as he was pleased to bestow it. This is why the Scripture says: "When he

went up front he captivated the leadership; he gave men **gifts."**
Now when it says "he went up front" it implies he was also in **the**
rear, or the lower reaches of the earth. This same one who **was**
in the rear also assumed the spiritual leadership and is in **charge**
of everything. The "gifts" which he made are appointments **as**
missionaries, preachers, reporters, organizers and educators, **who**
are to shape the believers into a working force, into a functioning
Christian body. Their job is not complete until we all come **into**
the oneness of the faith and the unifying experience of God's Son—
until we become grown men, filled out to the measurements **of**
Christ's size.

14. They are to help us quit being babies, so easily swayed **and**
carried away by every windbag that comes along with some **clever**
gimmick, with some big show to snare the gullible. Rather, **let us**
by practicing the truth in love, grow up in every way under **Christ**
our head. Under his leadership all the rest of the body is **coordi-**
nated and neatly fitted together with the necessary parts, **each**
functioning in its own way so as to give a lovely symmetry **to the**
whole body.

17. Now I want to say this to you, and I believe I'm **speaking**
for the Lord: Forever quit living like the rest of society who **live**
in the utter emptiness of their intellects with the shades of **their**
minds pulled down, complete foreigners to God's way of life. **They**
got this way through lack of insight and by spiritual **callousness.**
They are so greedy that God turned them loose in their stink **and**
let them run wild in their shameful brawls.

20. You all were *never* taught that such conduct was **Christian.**
On the contrary, if you really paid attention and were **instructed**
in the truth as Jesus gave it, then strip off the old rotten **clothes**
of your previous way of life, which was so full of lust and **deceit,**
and let the Spirit rejuvenate your mind and make you a new **per-**
son, created by God for righteousness and dedication and **truth.**

25. So then, let each one of you put away the false and speak only the truth to his brother, because we're all in this together. Don't sin by flying off the handle. Never let the sun set on a tantrum of yours, and don't give in one inch to the Devil. Let the man who has been in the habit of stealing cut it out. Let him go to work and make an honest living with his own hands, so he'll have something to share with the needy.

29. Let no off-color word fall from your lips. Instead, talk about any good thing needful for one's uplift, so that you'll benefit those listening. Don't wring the heart of God's Holy Spirit, who stamped his OK on you on your emancipation day.

31. Let every scrap of bitterness and resentment and anger and loud talk and running down of others be put away from you, along with all other evil. Deal gently with one another and maintain a good attitude. Show goodwill toward each other as God showed toward you in Christ.

5.

1. Therefore, become God's mimics, like children who are dearly loved. Make love a habit, just as Christ loved you and gave himself up for us as an offering and sacrifice to God like a fragrant perfume. Don't let sexual sins or any lewdness or money-grubbing even be mentioned among you, just as Christians ought to behave. Smutty jokes, dirty language and running off at the mouth aren't put up with either, only those things that are aboveboard. This should be absolutely clear to you that anybody who is sexually loose, or a punk, or a money-grubber has no place in God's and Christ's spiritual family. Don't let anybody kid you with slick talk. That's why God is mad at the people who have gone to the dogs. Don't let them suck you in. For you once operated under cover of darkness, but now in the Lord's light. Behave as people of light, for light produces only goodness and uprightness and truth. Test a thing to see if it is acceptable to the Lord, and don't participate in meaningless and shady activities. Instead, bring them out into the open, for the things some people do in secret are so shameful you can hardly talk about them. Everything that is exposed to the light is clearly visible, and that which is clearly visible is obviously on the side of light. That's why it says:

> Get up, you sleepyhead,
> And arise from the dead,
> And God's Son will bathe you in light.

15. Take extra care, then, how you live—not like nitwits but like wits. Use your time as though you had to buy it, because there's a lot of wickedness around these days. Therefore, don't be dumbbells but have an intelligent understanding of what the will of the Lord is. Don't get drunk on wine and carry on a lot of foolishness; tank up on the Spirit and do your talking to each other with hymns and songs and spirituals, singing and strumming in your hearts to the Lord. Always give thanks for everything to the Father-God in the name of our Lord Jesus Christ. Put yourselves under one another with Christ-like respect.

22. You women, be subject to your men as to the Lord, because a man is head of the woman just as Christ is head of the church and is himself the nerve center of the body. But as the church is subject to Christ, so also women are subject to men in everything.

25. You men, love your women, just as Christ loved the church and gave himself for her, so that, having bathed her in purity, like a bath in water, so to speak, he might stand her by his side, a lovely church without stain or dirt or anything like that, but that she might be true and pure. Men ought to love their women as though they were their own bodies. He who loves his own woman loves his own body. No one ever hates his own body, but rather he takes care of it and grooms it, just as Christ does the church, because we are parts of his body.

31. "For this reason a man shall sever his ties to Papa and Mama and shall be wrapped up in his woman, and the two will be a unified body." Admittedly, this whole thing is a puzzle—I mean Christ and the church. Anyway, you all—every one of you—love your woman as though she were you, and let the woman have respect for her man.

6.

1. You kids, listen to your parents,[2] for this is as it should be. "Respect your father and mother" is the first of the commandments with a promise attached—"that it might go well with you and you will live a long time on earth."

4. You fathers, don't aggravate your kids, but bring them up in the Lord's guidance and counsel.

5. You workers, cooperate with those over you with humility and respect and with the same kind of loyalty you give to Christ—not for praise or promotion, but as Christ's workers, doing the will of God from the heart and carrying out your work with a good attitude as though the Lord, and not man, were your employer. Realize that whether you are a worker or an employer, whatever good thing you do will be noticed by the Lord.

9. And you employers, treat your workers the same way. Don't go around breathing down their necks. Understand that both they and you have the same boss, the Lord in heaven, who makes no distinction between employer and employee.

10. Lastly, be strong and courageous men for Christ. Put on God's uniform so as to be able to withstand all the Devil's tricks. For we're not fighting against ordinary human beings, but against the leaders, politicians and heads of state of this dark world, against spiritual wickedness in high places. So, put on God's uniform so you'll be able to put up a fight on the day of battle and,

[2]Some reliable Greek manuscripts add "in the Lord."

having tended to every detail, to make your stand. Therefore, take your position when you have put on the pants of truth, the shirt of righteousness, and the shoes of the good news of peace. Above all, take the bulletproof vest of faith, with which you'll be able to stop the tracer bullets of the evil one. Also, wear the helmet of salvation, and the pistol of the Spirit, which is God's word.

18. When you offer a prayer or a petition on any occasion, let it be truly spiritual. Along this same line, be on your toes as you encourage and pray for all the members. Pray especially for me, that when I speak, the right words will be put in my mouth, and that I may boldly expound the gospel's secret, for which I am now a delegate in the clink. Pray too that I may lay it on the line whenever I have a chance to speak.

21. To let you all know how things are with me, and what I am doing, I've asked Tic, my dear brother and faithful assistant in the Lord, to tell you everything. This is the very reason I sent him to you—so he could give you the news about us, and that he might boost your spirits.

23. Peace to the brothers and love mixed with faith from the Father-God and the Lord Jesus Christ. May divine favor be upon all who unashamedly love our Lord Jesus Christ.

Yours,
Paul

The Letter to the Alabaster
African Church, Smithville, Alabama

[PHILIPPIANS]

1.

1. From two of Jesus Christ's slaves, Paul and Timothy;
To all the loyal Christians at Alabaster, especially the ministers and church officers.

Grace and peace to you from our Father-God and from our Master, Jesus Christ.

3. Every thought of you makes me thank God for you, and all my prayers for you are flooded with joy because of your partnership with me in the good news from the very first moment you heard it until the present. And I can assure you that, having started you off on the right track, I will follow through until Jesus Christ has his day. It is nothing but right that I should feel this way about you all, for I have a very warm spot in my heart for you. All of you are my fellow partners in God's grace, whether I'm in jail or preaching and explaining the gospel. I declare before God that I have the same tender feelings toward you as Christ Jesus himself does. And this I pray: that your love may keep growing until you have such understanding and keen perception that you can sort out the truly important matters. I pray too that you may overflow with the goodness that comes from following Christ, to God's credit and honor.

12. I want to let you know, brothers, that everything that has happened to me has actually advanced the gospel. For it is now quite clear to all the guards and to everybody else that I am in jail for my Christian convictions. Furthermore, my jailing has greatly strengthened most of the brothers in the Lord and they are daring to speak fearlessly the word of God. It is true, perhaps, that some are motivated by envy or even rivalry, but the others preach Christ from genuine conviction and love. They know that I am put here to make a clear case for the good news. They who insincerely preach Christ just to get a following of their own suppose that they will make my imprisonment all the more bitter. So what? Only that in every way, whether for outward show or genuine truth, Christ is proclaimed! I am glad about this, and will continue to be glad. I am certain that, with the help of your prayers and the continued support from the Spirit of Jesus Christ, this thing will actually make me better off spiritually. And I am confidently banking on the fact that I'll not be let down in the least. Whether I live or die, so long as there's a breath left in my body, even as previously and so now, I will boldly exalt Christ. For it is Christ if I live, and gain if I die. If I keep living, there must be something worthwhile for me to do. I just don't know which I'd rather do, because I am drawn by the prospects of both. I have a deep desire to set sail and be with Christ, for this is better by far. Yet for your sakes it is more urgent for me to stay on here. Since the latter seems certain, I guess I will stick around and lend you all a hand for the improvement and enjoyment of your faith. In this way you'll be all the more enthusiastic about Christ Jesus for my having come by to see you again.

27. The main thing is that your life together be becoming to Christ's gospel. Then, whether I get by to see you or am absent and hear only reports about you, I'll know that you stand as one man, carrying out with perfect teamwork the faith of the gospel. Do not be the least bit scared of those on the opposing team. Your fearlessness is proof to them of their failure and of your God-sent success. For to you it has been granted, on behalf of Christ, not only to walk in his way but also to suffer for him. Run the same race you saw me run and in which you hear that I am now engaged.

2.

1. So then, if there is a measure of mutual strength in Christ, a certain persuasiveness of love, a kind of spiritual partnership; if there is an element of genuine compassion and concern, make me completely happy by being harmonious, by having the same love, co-thinkers, people of a single purpose. Never act competitively or for self-praise, but with humbleness esteem others as above yourselves. Don't confine yourselves to your own interests, but seek the welfare of others. In this regard, you all think as Christ Jesus did. Though he was in a God form, he didn't think that being on an equality with God was something to be hoarded. So he humbled himself and took on a slave form, just like any other human being. And on purpose he turned up as a man and brought himself so low that he submitted to death—even a death on the gallows. That's why God is so proud of him and has bestowed on him the name that is above every name. In homage to the name of Jesus every knee on land, sky or sea shall bow, and every tongue shall cry out in praise to the Father-God, "JESUS CHRIST IS LORD."

12. So then, my loved ones, just as you've always been obedient, not only when I was with you but especially now that I'm absent, I urge you to carry on with your emancipation with a deep sense of reverence and responsibility. For it is God who gives you the energy both to will and to work in his behalf.

14. Do everything without griping and arguing, so as to be clean and above reproach, uncorrupted children of God in the midst of misguided and bad people, among whom you shine as beacons in the world, offering to all of them the living ideas. Then I'll be proud of you in the dawning Christian era, because you will be my proof that I neither ran in vain nor worked for nothing. For even if my life is sacrificed in ministering to your faith, I am glad and want to share my joy with you. And if you are called upon to do the same, you too rejoice and in turn share your joy with me.

19. As soon as possible I am hoping, with the permission of the Lord Jesus, to send Timothy to you so he can put my mind at ease about you. For I have no one else with a spirit like his, who will be so genuinely concerned about you. All the others are primarily interested in their own welfare, not the things of Christ Jesus. But you know his record, how he, like a son to his father, practically enslaved himself to me in the gospel. So I'll send him just as soon as I can find out how things will turn out for me here. I feel certain in the Lord that I myself will be coming to you in a little while.

25. Also, I consider it urgent to send to you Happy, my brother and co-worker and fellow soldier, whom you sent to wait on me during this time of need. He has been homesick for you all, and quite distressed because you heard that he was ill. Indeed he was so sick he nearly died. But God had mercy on him—not just on him but on me too—so I wouldn't have one grief on top of another. So I'll hurry up and send him, because when you see him again you will be happy and I'll be relieved. Give him a sure-enough joyful homecoming in the Lord, and hold men like him in high esteem, because he nearly died for the work of Christ. He actually risked his life pinch-hitting for you and lending me a helping hand.

3.

1. Finally, my brothers, be glad you are Christians. (Writing like this to you is no great chore for me, and it will do you no harm.) Be on your guard against "the dogs," against the bad actors, against religious racketeers. For *we* are the true church, that is, all who worship God spiritually, who stand up for Christ Jesus and who put no stock in status symbols—even though I myself have plenty of these symbols. If anybody else thinks he has status, I have even more—a baptized church member, a white man from an old Southern family, a 100 per cent Anglo-Saxon. As to religion, a Protestant; as to dedication, giving all outside agitators hell; as to church rules and regulations, spotless. But everything that was "profit" for me I put down as "loss" for Christ. Yes, indeed, I consider *everything* to be loss as over against the surpassing worth of the knowledge of Christ Jesus, my Lord. I lost everything for him and think of it as but garbage, that I might instead get Christ and identify myself with him, not having my own brand of church goodness but a goodness that comes through obedience to Christ, a God kind of goodness based on *obedience*. I did all this to get to know him, to have the astounding power of his Risen Presence, to be a partner with him in his sufferings. I committed myself to him in death, if somehow I might share in his aliveness. I don't claim that I have already arrived or that I am as yet fully mature. But I keep on struggling, trying to catch on to why Christ Jesus caught hold of me. Brothers, I don't think I've caught on even yet, but with this one thing in mind, forgetting everything that lies behind and concentrating on what lies ahead, I push on with all I've got toward the prize of God's invitation to the high road in Christ Jesus. So then, let all of us who are mature set our minds on this. Even if you should see things somewhat differently, this too will God make clear to you. Let's just live up to the progress we have already made.

17. Become my fellow mimics, brothers, and watch those who walk according to the example we set for you. For many people have joined the church, about whom I have frequently told you and even now am telling you with tears in my eyes that they are bitterly opposed to the thought of Christ's lynching. With their minds set only on material things, their destination is destruction, their god is pleasure, and their pride is in their shameful behavior. For *our* church fellowship is a spiritual thing, out of which we constantly expect the deliverer, the Lord Jesus Christ. He will transform our humble little group into a form resembling his own glorious body, by means of the inner working which enables him to captivate everybody.

4.

1. Now then, my loved and esteemed brothers, my pride and joy, hold the line for Christ, dear ones.

2. I beg Eunice and I beg Cindy to settle their differences in the spirit of the Lord. Yes, and I beg you too, my loyal and true buddy, to give a hand to those women who shared the gospel struggle with me and Clement and my other co-workers, whose names are inscribed on the "Scroll of Life."

4. Always be glad you are Christians. I say it again, be glad. Let your gentleness show through to *all* people. The Lord is close by, so don't fret over anything. Rather, as you thankfully pray, let God in on all your needs. Then God's peace, which is beyond anything you have ever experienced, will stand watch over your mind and emotions in Christ Jesus.

8. Lastly, brothers, all that's true, all that's honorable, all that's right, all that's clean, all that's friendly, and all that's uplifting— if you are looking for something genuine and worthwhile, consider *these things.* And keep on practicing all that I taught you and demonstrated to you and told you and showed you. And the God of peace will be with you.

10. As a member of the fellowship, I am truly glad that you are now concerned about me. You've had me in mind all along, but were unable to show it. I'm not hinting that I'm in need, for actually I've learned the secret of both feasting and fasting, of being loaded and being broke. With the help of him who empowers me, I feel up to *anything.*

14. But just the same, it surely was good of you to share as partners with me in my troubles. For you yourselves know, my Alabaster friends, that in the earliest days of the gospel, when I left Alabama, not one single fellowship joined with me in the common purse for mutual sharing except you alone. For even while I was in Mississippi, you sent money time and again to meet my needs. It's not that I'm looking for a handout, but I am expecting the kind of action from you that will increasingly enrich *you.*

18. I received everything in good shape and am bursting at the seams. Ever since I got the stuff you sent by Happy, I have been brimful. Your gift is like sweet perfume, a noble sacrifice, pleasing to God. May my God meet your every need in keeping with his marvelous wealth displayed in Christ Jesus. And may the credit be given to our Father-God through all ages. Please may it be so.

21. Greet every person dedicated to Christ Jesus. The brothers here with me ask to be remembered to you. In fact, all the Christians here, particularly the government workers who have joined us, send you their warm greetings.

23. May the unmerited favor of the Lord Jesus Christ be with your spirit.

Yours,
Paul

The Letter to the Christians
in Columbus [COLOSSIANS]

1.

1. From Paul, by God's will a minister of Jesus Christ, and
Brother Timothy;
To the dedicated and faithful Christian brothers in Columbus.

2. We wish you peace and the best of everything from our
Father-God. Every time we pray we surely do thank the Father-
God of our Lord Jesus for you all. We have heard about the way
you live for Jesus Christ and the love you show toward all the believers. It's a sign of your sureness on essential spiritual matters.
You first learned of this when the true word of the gospel was
presented to you, and it is now multiplying and bearing fruit all
over the world the same as it has been doing in you ever since you
were privileged to hear and understand God's truth. It's the same
as you learned it from our good old buddy, Pat, who is as loyal a
Christian friend as you ever had. He's the one who convinced us,
by his spirit, of your love. From that moment on we haven't let up
praying for you all. We are asking that in every scrap of wisdom
and spiritual insight you might be loaded up with a clear understanding of what God is up to, and thus behave in a way that's
pleasing to the Lord. May you shuck out every kind of good deed
and bust out all over with the true understanding of God. In everything that demands strength, may you have the energy of his marvelous dynamo to give you all the patience and persistence you

need. And may you give joyful thanks to the Father who enabled you to be partners with enlightened Christians.

13. It was the Father who sprang us from the jailhouse of darkness, and turned us loose in the new world of his beloved Son, through whom we got our pardon, the forgiveness of our crimes. He is a perfect photo of the Unseen God, and has got it over everything that ever was made, because he's the reason everything was put together, whether it's in heaven or on earth, whether seen or unseen, whether sitting on thrones or governors' chairs, on judges' benches or in sheriffs' offices. Through him and for him the whole business has been put together. He's the starting point of everything, and he's got it all in the palm of his hand. Too, he is the boss of the body, his church. He is the source, the originator of the resurrection. The result is that he's tops any way you look at it. In him God put all his eggs in one basket and showed, through him, that he was friendly towards everybody. Indeed, by the blood shed at his lynching he brought about peace with all, both on the earth and in heaven.

21. At one time you all were not on speaking terms with God, and because of your mean ways, you had your mind set dead against him. But now, by dying he has made friends of you who are in his visible body, so as to get you on your feet before him—dedicated, clean and above reproach. But you've gotta stay with the faith, riding it out and staying in the saddle without getting bucked off the back of the gospel—the gospel which you yielded to and of which I, Paul, am an agent.

24. Now I am quite happy that by suffering for you I am able to extend in my flesh the incompleted afflictions of Christ for his body, which is the church. I became his agent by the divine appointment which was given to me, so as to bring God's word to a head in you. This indeed is the secret which has been hidden away for ages and generations and has now been made public in those who are dedicated to him. In them God wanted to exhibit among all races what a priceless thing this glorious mystery is, the mystery of Christ's indwelling presence with you all, the basis of the glory. It's *him* we keep talking about. We spur people on and teach everybody with all the wisdom we've got so as to help every man stand on his own two feet as a grown-up Christian. To this end I work like a dog, straining with all the energy which he so powerfully released in me.

2.

1. I'd like you to know what a deep concern I have for you, as well as for everybody in Montgomery and for all whom I've never personally met. I'm anxious that their hearts, yoked together in love and in the good fortune of a full-blown awakening, might be boosted into an awareness of God's mystery—Christ himself. For in him, still unexplored, are all the values of education and wisdom. I say this so nobody will trip you with their smooth talk. For even though I'm not actually present, my spirit is with you, and it it really sends me to see your orderliness and your firmness in the Christian faith.

6. Keep on walking in Christ Jesus the Lord just as when you first received him. Sink your roots in him; bet your life on him; plant your feet firmly in the faith as you were taught it; bubble over with joyful thanks.

8. Watch your step now and don't let anybody make a sucker of you with his intellectual jazz and his smooth-sounding baloney, which is based on human concoctions and worldly standards, not on Christ. For the whole spectrum of Deity resided corporately in him, in whom your own lives find meaning. He's the boss over every ruler and big shot. And by him you've been initiated into his fellowship—I don't mean physical initiation—when he relieved you of your lower nature. This indeed is Christian initiation. Likewise, in baptism you were buried with him, and with him you have been raised by the inner working of faith in God who raised him from the dead. And to you all, corpses rotting in your sins and moral estrangement, God gave new life along with him. He freely forgave all our wrongdoing; he scratched out the signed charges against us which were then pending, took them out of the courtroom and tied *them* in the noose! And having frisked the top brass and the power boys, and made them his prisoners of war, he publicly exposed them.

16. Therefore, don't ever let one of those big shots jump all over you about official regulations or special observances or denominational programs or Sunday activities. Such things are but *forms*, whereas Christ is the real stuff. And don't let anybody browbeat you into an assumed piety and into prayers to saints, insisting on some vision he has had. He's a worldly-minded muddlehead who has lost his grip on the true Head, under which the rest of the body, outfitted and bound together by its joints and muscles, grows into God's maturity.

20. If with Christ you died off from the standards of the world, why do you keep insisting on the world's way of living? "Keep away from such-and-such"; "Don't drink that"; "Hands off this." These are all perishable things, and the rules and teachings regarding them are purely human. Sure, it all sounds terrific with its daily devotions, its self-commitment and its rigorous disciplines, but it isn't worth a hoot to anybody who wants to live above a human level.

3.

1. So then, if you've been given new life in Christ, go after the things of the New Order, in which Christ rules with God's authority. Set your hearts on the ways of the New Order, not on those of the world. For you all *died,* and your Christian life is now wrapped up in God. Whenever Christ—our life—is made real, then you too shall be made real with him in a wonderful way.

5. That's why you should kill off those areas of your life which are worldly, such as whoring, gutterbugging, uncontrolled emotions, wicked craving, and being too rich, which is false worship. These are the things which bring down God's wrath. And at one time, when you were living in the old ways, you yourselves practiced such things. But now you all must have no truck with all that nor with blowing your top, getting all steamed up, acting ugly, throwing your weight around and running off at the mouth with dirty jokes. Quit playing false with one another, since you have shucked off the old man and his habits, and have put on the new one which is constantly being remade to the specifications of its Creator's pattern. The pattern for the new man is the same for a Negro and a white man, a church member and non-church-member, foreigner, Mexican, employee, employer, but Christ is everything in everybody.

12. Wear the clothes, then, that will identify you as people whom God has selected and dedicated and loved. Your outfit should include a tender heart, kindness, genuine humility, loyalty, persistence. Put up with one another, and freely forgive each other if one has a gripe against somebody. You all forgive as freely as the Lord forgave you. Over all these things wear love, which is the robe of maturity. And let Christ's peace, into which you were called as one fellowship, order your lives. And be thankful for it. Let Christ's nature find abundant lodging among you. Teach and correct each other with great wisdom. With joy in your hearts sing hymns and songs and spirituals to God. And no matter what you're doing, by word or deed, let everything be in the name of the Lord Jesus, all the while giving thanks through him to the Father-God.

18. Ladies, be subordinate to your men, as becomes a Christian wife. Men, love your wives and don't act ornery toward them. Kids, always obey your parents, for this pleases the Lord. Fathers, don't dominate your kids too much lest their spirits be broken. Employees, always cooperate with your human bosses, not for promotion or praise, but with the pure motive which springs from reverence for God. Whatever you do, do it from the heart, as though you were working for God and not men. You may rest assured that you will receive from the Lord the pay that's due you. You are employed by Christ the Lord. For the crook will get back his own crookedness, since there is no favoritism.

4.

1. Employers, treat your employees with justice and equality, realizing that you yourselves have a spiritual employer.

2. Keep saying your prayers, and when you do, stay awake on the thanksgiving. Also, please pray for us, that God might open for us a door to preach, to explain the Christian secret, for which I've been arrested. Pray that when I speak I may lay it on the line as I ought to. Walk sensibly before outsiders, using your time as though you had to buy it. Let your conversation always be graceful and properly seasoned, so you'll know how you should respond to others.

7. My dear buddy Tic, my faithful helper and co-worker in the Lord, will share the news about me with you all. In fact, I sent him to you for just this reason, so you might be brought up to date on the happenings on this end, and that he might pep you up a bit. With him is Obie, our loyal and loved brother, who is a member of your congregation. They'll fill you in on all the details here.

10. Rusty, my fellow jail-bird, sends his greetings to you, as does Mark, Barney's cousin. (You received instructions about him that if he came your way you should take him in.) Greetings also from Josh, or Justus as he is called. These are the only whites who are my partners in the God movement. They have become a tower of strength to me. Pat, another of your members, also greets you. An utterly devoted Christian, he is always agonizing over you in his prayers, that you may stand mature and fully equipped in the total will of God. For I know for a fact that he is heavily burdened for you and for those in Montgomery and Mobile. Luke, the beloved doctor, and Damon want to be remembered to you. Give our greetings to the brothers from Montgomery, and to Nancy and the church gathered at her house.

16. When you've finished reading this letter, send it over to the Montgomery church for them to read, and get the one they have so you can read it. And tell Arch: "Be careful to carry out the assignment you got from the Lord."

18. The greeting is in my own handwriting. Remember my chains.

> Best wishes to you all,
> *Paul*

The First Letter to the
Selma Christians [I THESSALONIANS]

1.

1. From Paul, Silas and Timothy;
To the fellowship of Selma folks who are rooted in Father-God
and in Lord Jesus Christ.
Grace and Peace to you.

2. We unceasingly thank God for you all and are continually
bringing you up in our prayers. And in the presence of our Father-
God we recall how you lived by your faith, put your love to work,
and stuck by your hope in our Lord Jesus Christ. My brothers
whom God loves, you may be sure of your prize. For our great story
was not brought to you in sermons alone, but in powerful action, in
a dedicated spirit, and in much forthrightness. Well, you know
the kind of guys we were while working with you and for you,
because you yourselves imitated us and the Lord. With the joy of
a dedicated spirit, you accepted the word and paid a terrific price
so that you became a challenge to all the believers in Mississippi
and Alabama. For from you the word of the Lord has echoed not
only in Mississippi and Alabama but all over the country. News of
the way you live for God is so widespread that we don't need to
bring it up any more. Others are now telling about what kind of
visit we had with you, and how you switched from your old sacred
customs to God; in fact, how you literally enslaved yourselves to
the true and living God and practiced the presence of his Risen
Son, Jesus, whom he made to live again and who keeps on getting
us out of the damnation that's always pressing in on us.

2.

1. Brothers, you yourselves know that our visit with you was no tea party. You also know that just before this we got beat up and cussed out in Smithville. Just the same, we were given the courage by our God to preach the word of God to you, knowing we would get into a lot of trouble. For our approach is not to beat around the bush nor to get in the mud ourselves nor to be sneaky; rather, since we have been examined by God to be fit to handle the gospel, we speak, not to be popular, but to be responsible to God, who constantly inspects our hearts. For never once did we soft-soap anybody, as you well know, nor pretend to have a lot of money—God knows—nor try to extract praise from people—from either you or anybody else. As Christian missionaries we had the right to free-load on you, but instead, all the while with you we were as thoughtful of you as a good baby-sitter taking care of her children. With such fussy concern over you, we were glad to share with you not only the gospel of God but even our very lives, because we had come to love you very, very much. Brothers, just review our sweat and our grubbing. Moonlighting so as not to freeload on any of you, we preached God's good news among you. You can testify and so can God as to how dedicated and right and above reproach our lives were with you believers. You know, like a father talking to his own boy we counseled with each one of you, sharing our insights and showing you how to walk becomingly of the God who called us into his movement and magnificence.

13. And another reason why we keep thanking God continually is that, having listened to the word of God spoken by us, you accepted it not as man's reasoning but, as it truly is, *God's* reasoning, which even now is energizing you who are living by it. For brothers, you all became exactly like God's Christian fellowships in Georgia, because you suffered the very same things at the hands of your kinfolks as the Georgia Christians did from their fellow whites who lynched the Lord Jesus and the honest preachers. They gave us hell too, and couldn't have cared less about God. With

utter contempt for human beings they ordered us not to tell the
Negroes how to be helped. As always, they piled their sins sky-
high, and damnation got on their tails before it was over.

17. So, brothers, having been separated from you for a while
(physically, that is, not spiritually) we have been all the more
anxious to see you in person. Once, and then again, we—or rather
I, Paul—tried to get by to see you but Satan blocked the way. For
who but you is our hope, our joy, our crown of authority before
our Lord Jesus in his movement? Yes, indeed, *you all* are our pride
and joy!

3.

1. Well, when our separation from you reached the breaking
point, we decided that I should stay on alone in Hattiesburg, and
we sent Timothy, our brother and God's partner in the gospel of
Christ, to put some steel in your spirit and to pep up your faith
so nobody would get cold feet from all these acts of violence. For
you realize that this is all part of the game, because while we were
with you we kept warning you that we would be given the works.
And sure enough, that's what happened, as you now know. That's
why, when I just couldn't take it any more, I sent to find out what
was happening to your faith, fearing that possibly the Confuser
was confusing you and that our effort there might be lost.

6. But a little while ago Timothy got here from you and brought
us the good news about your faith and love. He told us that you
always have a high opinion of us, and that you're as hungry to see
us as we are to see you. I tell you, brothers, your faith surely
meant a lot to us in our own difficulties and troubles. With you
standing up for the Lord we can now start breathing again. Oh,
how can we ever thank God enough for all the joy you've brought
us in the presence of our God! And oh, how we're praying around
the clock to catch a glimpse of your face and to fill in the gaps of
your faith! May our Father-God himself and our Lord Jesus home

us in on you! May the Lord load you up and run you over with love for one another and for everybody else too, the same as we have for you. May you have the guts to stand without reservation and in utter abandonment before our Father-God in the Inauguration of our Lord Jesus, in company with all those who are devoted to him.

4.

1. So finally, brothers, in order that you might grow even more, we beg you and plead with you in the Lord Jesus to keep on walking exactly as you learned from us how one who would please God must walk. For you are aware of the various instructions we gave you with the help of the Lord Jesus. God's will—that which makes you different—is that you hold back from catting around, that each of you know how to control his own genitals with dedication and honor, not with lustful passion like those guys who don't know God; and that one not go over and stimulate his brother in this matter. Just as we told you before and keep on mentioning it to you, the Lord is ruthless toward all such things. For God called us not for loose living but in disciplined dedication. And so then, the rebel is rebelling not against man but against the God who gives you his Holy Spirit.

9. Now you don't need me to write you about brotherly love, because you yourselves are God-taught to love one another. And you are doing just this toward all the brothers even throughout Mississippi. But we are encouraging you to grow even more in this respect—also to consider it a virtue to keep your ears, not your mouth, open and to tend to your own business, and earn your living, just as we strictly ordered you, so that your conduct will appeal to those outside the fellowship and that you yourselves not go hungry.

13. Now we don't want you to be in the dark, brothers, about those who have died, lest your grief be the same as those who have no hope. For if we believe that Jesus died and was made to live, then just as surely will God bring to life, through Jesus, those who have died with him. Now this we say to you on the authority of the Lord: We who remain alive in the Lord's movement shall in no way get a head start on those Christians who have died. For the Lord himself, at countdown, with a sound like a big angel and God Almighty blowing a siren, will blast off from heaven. And the dead Christians will come to life first, then we who are still living will be whooshed up in the clouds with them to meet the Lord in the sky. Then we shall live happily with the Lord ever after. So use these words to calm down one another.

5.

1. Brothers, you don't have any need for me to write to you about schedules and seasons. For you yourselves know for a fact that "Lord's Day" comes like somebody breaking in at night. Just when people settle back and say, "It's so peaceful and quiet," then all of a sudden calamity hits them like a woman having labor pains, and then it's too late. But you all, my brothers, are not *night* creatures with the *day* about to surprise you as a thief. You all are *light* children; you are *daytime* people; we don't belong to the night nor to darkness. Well, then, let's not wallow around in bed like other people but let's keep moving and stay on our toes. For sleepers sleep of a night, and drunkards get drunk of a night. But let us, since we are daytime people, get on the ball. Let's put on the space suit of faith and love, and the headgear of hope and salvation. Because God has not intended damnation for us but an achievement of salvation through our Lord Jesus Christ. He died for us, that whether we wake or sleep, we shall surely live with him. Therefore, stand by one another and each one build up the other, just as you are doing now.

12. We call on you, brothers, to recognize those who are slaving for you and are your managers and trainers in the Lord. Show them particular affection because of their work. Cultivate peace among yourselves. We encourage you, brothers, to straighten out the cantankerous, lend a hand to the spiritual runts, doctor the sickly, and get along with everybody. See that no one pays back another evil for evil, but always press for the good in one another and in everybody. Always be cheerful. Never quit praying. Be thankful for everything, for this is God's will for you.

Don't switch off the Spirit.

Don't belittle honest preaching.

Sample things, accept what's good and reject every hint of evil.

23. May the very God of peace totally possess you. May he make one bundle of your spirit, mind and body and keep you above reproach in the movement of our Lord Jesus Christ. You can trust him who called us to do this.

25. Brothers, keep us in your prayers. Greet all the brothers with our heartfelt love.

I put you under oath to the Lord that you read this letter to all the brothers.

May the unmerited favor of our Lord Jesus Christ be with you.

Paul, Silas and Timothy

The Second Letter to the Christians in Selma

[II THESSALONIANS]

1.

1. From Paul, Silas and Timothy;
To the fellowship of Selma folks who are rooted in our Father-God and in Lord Jesus Christ.
Grace and peace to you from Father-God and Lord Jesus Christ.

3. We feel bound to thank God continually for you, brothers, which is nothing but right. Your faith is growing and the love of each one of you for one another is getting bigger and bigger. Why, we ourselves are singing your praise throughout God's fellowships, telling about your tenacity and faith in the face of all your persecutions, and the terrible things you're putting up with. It's an indication of the rightness of God's decision to count you worthy of his movement[1] for which you are suffering so. It would be only right if God dished out some trouble to those troubling you, and gave a breathing spell for you and us who are being mistreated. It'll happen, too, on that day when Lord Jesus, with his mighty angels about him, will bust out of the spiritual realm and with roaring fire will mete out justice to those who ignore God and won't live by the gospel of our Lord Jesus. They'll be sentenced to spiritual exile from the presence of the Lord and from the mighty display when he shall come to be honored by his devout ones and to be amazed himself at all the believers. Because our

---

[1]The Greek word is "kingdom."

position on this was accepted by you we are always praying for you, that our God may make you worthy of the call and may make a reality of every intention of goodness and every work undertaken in the power of faith, so that the Name of our Lord Jesus may be held in honor by you, and you by him, according to the unmerited favor of our God and Lord Jesus Christ.

2.

1. Brothers, let us speak earnestly to you about the *coup*[2] of our Lord and our gathering together around him, so that you may not be easily thrown for a loop nor upset by a "spirit" or a message or a letter supposed to be from us stating that the Lord's era[3] has "arrived."[4] Don't let anybody bag you with that kind of foolish-- ness. For unless there first comes the reformation,[5] and the mask is pulled off the Man of Tyranny, the damned bastard, who opposes and lords it over everything called God or sacred; in fact, he sits in God's house and claims that he himself *is* God . . .[6] Don't you re- member that while I was with you I was telling you these things? Even now you know the Despot, so he may be unmasked in his own time. For already the secret of tyranny is working only until the Despot can be gotten out of the way. And then the Tyrant shall

---

[2]The word here is παρουσία, "appearance" or "presence." Here it seems to indicate the sudden appearance of one leading a *coup*.

[3]The Greek word is "day" but it can refer to a period, or age, or era, as in our "day of the automobile." Thus Paul's thought is that while Christ's era reaches into the past and is also a present reality, it is not yet over. It stretches toward its future consummation. Its root is in the past; its trunk, in the present; its crown, in the future.

[4]Or "is an accomplished fact," "has fully dawned and has run its course," "has had its day," the implication being that it is now the "post-Christian" era. The verb is third person singular, perfect indicative of ἐνίστημι, "to be present," and represents the action as having been completed. The "train" has arrived, reached its destination, and will go no further. The action is over. It is a past event. We are done with it.

[5]The word is ἀποστησία (English "apostasy") and refers to a revolt, primarily a religious one; hence, reformation.

[6]Paul does not complete this sentence.

be unmasked and the Lord Jesus will smash him with a sneeze and make him powerless for the ushering in of HIS *coup*.[7] His *coup* is the result of Satan's energy expressed in much activity and charts and phony programs and in much crooked slick talk by those who are going to hell because they spurned the love of the truth whereby they may have been rescued. And that's why God is bringing upon them a "generator of error" that leads them to put stock in the outright lie, so that all who don't trust the truth but delight in wickedness might be brought to judgment.

13. Now my brothers whom the Lord loves, we should be forever grateful to God for you, because God chose you, by the dedication of your spirit and your trust of the truth, to lead the Freedom Parade. He also called you, through our preaching, to be an ornament of our Lord Jesus Christ. So then, brothers, stand your ground, and sink your teeth into the lessons we taught you, both orally and by letter. And may our Lord Jesus Christ personally, and our Father-God who by his grace loved us and gave us a charge that's out of this world and who provided us with a solid footing—may he charge your hearts and pep you up in every good deed and word.

3.

1. Lastly, brothers, pray for us, that the Christian faith may spread rapidly and be respected even as it has and is with you. Pray also that we may not fall into the hands of extreme [or unbalanced] and evil men, for not all are Christians. Surely the Lord will put starch into you and guard you against evil. And we have no doubt whatsoever that you are doing and will continue to do as we tell you. And may the Lord home your hearts in on the love of God and on the steadfastness of Christ.

---

[7] Παρουσία, the same word as in v. 1. Thus the world is faced with the prospect of TWO *coups*, that of the Lord and that of the Tyrant. But the outcome is already certain.

6. On the authority of the Lord Jesus Christ, we direct you, brothers, to part company with every brother who bucks out of the harness and refuses to live by the instructions you got from us. For you yourselves know how important it is to imitate us, because while we were with you we didn't buck out of the harness nor freeload on anybody. Instead, in hard labor and sweat we worked far into the night so as not to be a burden on any of you. It wasn't that we didn't have the *right* to eat off of you, but that we might set ourselves as an example for you to copy. For even while we were with you we kept insisting that if a man were unwilling to work he shouldn't come for chow. Now we hear that some there are not pulling their load, working at nothing but getting out of work. We are both ordering and urging those guys to quietly go to work and earn their own bread.

13. Brothers, don't you all ever lose your zest when you're doing what's right. And if anyone doesn't do what we've said in our letter, single him out and don't associate with him, so he'll be ashamed of himself. In other words, treat him, not as an enemy, but as a brother to be corrected. Now may the Lord of peace personally give you peace—always and in all ways. The Lord be with you all.

17. Now the greeting, written in my (Paul's) own hand, which is the way I sign every letter. Thus I am writing: *The grace of our Lord Jesus Christ be with you all.*

Paul, Silas and Timothy

The First Letter to Timothy

1.

1. From Paul, an agent of Jesus Christ by appointment of both our Savior-God and Jesus Christ, our hope;
 To Timothy, a legitimate child in the Christian faith.
 I wish you much favor, kindness and peace from our Father-God and our Lord Jesus Christ.

3. When I set out for Mississippi, I urged you to stay on in Birmingham so you could warn certain people not to spread wrong ideas nor get bogged down in endless programs and reports which generate a lot of discussion but little else for God's household of faith. The purpose of such a warning is to produce love which springs from a clean heart, a clear conscience and a sincere faith. A few of them, having missed the mark entirely, have soared off in high-flown gobbledygook. They want to be doctors of divinity, but they have no understanding of what they're talking about or what they're trying to prove.

8. Now we know that hellfire preaching is all right if one treats it as such, realizing that brimstone is not aimed at a truly good man but at the wild and unruly, the anti-religious and sinners, the holy Joes and the nice Nellies, the bombers of men, women and children, the catters, homos, exploiters, liars, fixers and anything else that's opposed to the wholesome teachings found in our blessed God's wonderful gospel with which I'm entrusted.

12. I am eternally grateful to our Lord Jesus Christ who cranked me up and considered me fit to be put into service. I used to be a slanderer, a persecutor and an insulter of Christians. But I was pitied, because as a disbeliever I did it without knowing what I was up to. And so the undeserved favor of our Lord just busted loose all over me, along with the faith and love for which Christ Jesus is famous. Timothy, you can bet your last dollar on this: *Christ Jesus came into the world to rescue sinners, and I'm the worst one of all.* But that's why I was pitied—that of me, the worst one, Christ Jesus might make Exhibit A of all his incredible goodwill. He used me as a display of what can happen to those who put their trust in him for spiritual life. So all honor and credit for evermore to the Leader of movements, undying, unseen, God alone. May it ever be so.

18. Timothy, my boy, in keeping with earlier predictions about you which enabled you to put up a sure-enough fight, I am entrusting to you this responsibility. Hold on to your faith and keep your conscience clean. Some people, among whom are Henry and Alec, have stifled their conscience and shipwrecked their faith. I let Satan have them, so they might learn not to play fast and loose with God.

2.

1. So in the first place, I recommend that requests, prayers, pleadings and thanksgivings be made for all people, for heads of state and for all who are in positions of authority, so that we might carry on a pleasant and quiet business with all reverence and dignity. This is proper and fitting before our Savior-God, who is anxious for all people to be rescued and to know what the truth really is. For God is one, and there is one connecting link between God and man—the Man Christ Jesus. *He sacrificed his own life as the price of setting all men free,* a fact that has become clear time and again. I was made a preacher and agent to spread this word, yes, and—believe it or not, but I'm telling the honest truth—*a teacher of other races* in the Christian faith and truth.

8. I'd like, then, for the men at each place to join in prayer, doing so with clean hands, with no hard feelings or arguments. It's also my wish that the women outfit themselves in suitable clothing with modesty and good taste. They should not go in for fancy hairdos and gold ornaments or expensive dresses, but for that which really becomes dedicated Christian women—their gracious ways. Let a woman learn to quietly take a subordinate place. I don't permit a woman to teach a man or to boss him but to stay in the background. For Adam (man) was put together first, then Eve (woman). And it was not Adam but Eve who was tricked and became the offender. But she'll get off the hook by having children, provided, of course, she shows good sense and lives in faith, love and devotion.

3.

1. You can bank on the fact that if a fellow seeks the office of overseer in the church, he has his heart set on an honorable occupation. It's necessary, therefore, that the overseer be a top-notch man, faithfully married to his wife, level-headed, with a lot of horse sense, polished, one who loves people, open-minded. He should not be an alcoholic, nor a military man, but gentle, nonviolent and free from the love of money. He should do a good job of running his own household and should show good judgment in keeping his children well in hand. (For if a man doesn't know how to manage his own home, how shall he take care of God's family?) He should not be a newcomer, lest he get the bighead and the Devil throw him for a loop. He must also be highly regarded by those outside the church, or the Devil might hook him with some scandal.

8. In the same way, the church's financial administrators[1] should be conscientious, straight-shooting, not hitting the bottle

---

[1]The word here is "deacon" and refers to those men appointed by the church to be responsible for the physical needs of the members. They were to see that none had too little—or too much!

very often, nor grubbing for money. They should hold onto the secret of the Christian faith without any reservations. Let them first serve a trial period and then if they pan out OK let them have the job. It's important, too, that their wives be conscientious, not devilish nor flightly, utterly loyal. Financial administrators must be faithfully married to their wives, handling well both their children and entire households. For they who serve well as financial administrators earn a fine reputation for themselves as well as much openness on matters of the Christian faith.

14. I'm writing these things to you in the hope that I'll be coming your way soon. But if I should be delayed, then you'll know how people must order their lives in the household of God, which is the Living God's family, the focal point and repository of the truth. And without doubt the secret of the Good Life is tremendous:

> Born in the flesh,
> Matured in the Spirit—
> While the angels peeped—
>
> Preached to all races,
> Trusted by the world,
> Returned to glory.

4.

1. The Spirit definitely tells us that as time moves on some people will twist Christianity out of shape. They'll go wild over misguided preachers and the books of distinguished devils. With their consciences branded with a hot iron, they hypocritically preach what isn't so. They teach that it is wrong to marry, and to eat certain foods which God made for believers and others who have an understanding of the truth to eat with humble gratitude. For all of God's creation is good, and nothing we gratefully accept is forbidden, since it is made kosher by God's work and intervention.

6. As you lay these things on the hearts of the brothers you will be a worthy agent of Christ Jesus, nourished on the ideas of the Christian faith and the fine principles which you've practiced. But don't get involved in ridiculous and seedy religious fads. Rather, give yourself a good workout in real religion. Physical fitness is quite valuable, but spiritual fitness is worth more than anything, because it enables one to have life for both the present and the future. Bank on this and don't hesitate to accept it. This is why we work and sweat, because we *have* bet our lives on the Living God, who is the rescuer of *all* peoples, and especially Christians.

11. Stress these things and teach them. Don't let anybody look down his nose at you just because you're a young man. Instead, you be an example of what church members should be in speech, in conduct, in love, in faith, in dedication. Till I come, keep up your reading, your counseling, your teaching. Care for the inner spiritual gift which was prophetically bestowed on you when the elders laid their hands on you. Let these things consume you; breathe them, so that it will be clear to everybody that you're making progress. Keep a tight check on yourself and your teaching. Stay on the ball, for by so doing you will save both yourself and those who listen to you.

5.

1. Don't jump all over an elder; rather, approach him as a father. Approach young men as brothers, elderly women as mothers and young women as sisters—in complete sincerity.

3. Accept responsibility for widows who are clearly dependent. If a widow has children or grandchildren, they should learn to exercise religion first at home and meet the needs of the elder members of the family, for this is what God expects. But a truly dependent widow who is alone pins her hopes on God and lives by asking and praying to him night and day. On the other hand, the widow that's revving it up, though she's living high now, has already died off. So insist on these things, that they may be above reproach. Too, if someone does not provide for his own relatives and especially his own family, he has denied the Christian faith and is really worse than a non-Christian. Now to get a pension from the church a widow must be at least sixty years old, undivorced, with a good reputation. You should know whether she reared her children well, if she was hospitable, if she put herself at the disposal of the church, if she befriended people in trouble, if she did all the good she could in every way. But turn down young widows. For when they get too hot for Christian restraint, their desire is to mate. Then they feel guilty for having broken their original commitment. But on top of this they learn to be loafers, flitting around to people's houses, not only loafing but babbling and carrying on like mad, never discussing anything important. So I recommend that the young widows get married, have children, keep house and not give someone opposed to us any grounds for ridiculing us. For already some have gone trekking off after Satan.

16. If a church member has widows in the family, let him provide for them and not burden the church, so it can provide for widows who are truly dependent.

17. Spiritual leaders who perform their duties well should be eligible for a double allotment, particularly those who make real sacrifices to preach and teach. For the Bible says, "Don't put a muzzle on a mule that's plowing corn," and, "A worker is entitled to his wages."

19. Don't entertain a charge against a spiritual leader unless there are two or three witnesses to back it up.

20. Openly rebuke those who make sin a habit, so as to put the fear of God into the rest.

21. I hereby call on you, in the presence of God and Christ Jesus and the chosen angels, to uphold these things with an unprejudiced mind and show no favoritism whatsoever. Don't embrace a fellow too quickly, nor be a partner with others in their sins; keep yourself clean. You may stop being a teetotaler, but use only a little wine to settle your stomach and for your serious illnesses.

6.

1. Let all who are laborers consider their bosses as worthy of the utmost respect so that God's name and Christian principles might not be smeared. Nor should workers whose bosses are church members and loved ones have hatred for them, since they are brothers. Rather, they should work all the harder, because the beneficiaries of a job well done are fellow church members and loved ones. Keep on teaching and counseling these things.

3. If anybody contradicts and does not consent to the sound principles laid down by our Lord Jesus Christ and to the well-tested precepts he gave, that man is a puffed up blowhard. He not only doesn't know the score, but he is cracked on side issues and controversial matters which give rise to hard feelings, breakups, smears and malicious suspicions. This is the kind of running off at the mouth that men do when their mind is festered and they've robbed the truth of all meaning. They're counting on getting well off on religion. The religion that produces *inner satisfaction* really *is* something to get well on. For we brought nothing into the world, and we surely can't take anything out of it. We have enough food and clothing, and with these we shall be content. You know, when people make money their goal they fall head over heels into confusion and into a bear trap and into all kinds of senseless and harmful cravings which shove them down into ruin and destruction. For the root of everything wicked is money-addiction. And some folks, in forming the habit, have ceased to be Christians and have hanged themselves with a peck of troubles.

11. But you, God's man, turn your back on all that. Set your heart on justice, honest religion, faith, love, steadiness, unswerving loyalty. Put all you've got into the faith's noble struggle. Stand on tiptoe to get the spiritual life into which you were invited and which you so nobly accepted in front of many others who had done the same thing. Before the God who makes all things alive and before Christ Jesus who made the Great Acceptance in front of Governor Pontius Pilate, I plead with you to keep the new commandment untainted and without compromise until our Lord Jesus Christ shows up. This will be made clear at his own convenience by the wonderful and only ruler, the President of presidents and the Governor of governors, who alone is deathless, whose home is blinding light, at which no human being has ever been able to look or ever will. To him be eternal respect and rule. May it ever be so.

17. Plead with the worldly rich not to be conceited nor to rest any weight on the mirage of wealth, but on God who liberally offers us everything needful for our well-being. Plead with them to do good, to be rich in noble deeds, to be sharers, full partners, assembling material for a fine foundation for the future, so that they might hang on to life that's real.

20. Timothy, guard your directions with your life. Don't get bogged down in the muddle-headed spoutings and fancy froth parading under the name of "higher learning." Some people have gone for that junk and have really messed up their Christian faith.

Best wishes to you all,
Paul

The Second Letter to Timothy

1.

1. From Paul, an agent of Jesus Christ appointed by God to carry through on the promise of the life seen in Christ Jesus;

To my dear son, Timothy. I wish you much favor, kindness and peace from Father-God and Christ Jesus, our Lord.

3. I breathe a word of thanks to God, whom I learned from my parents to serve with a clean conscience, when, without fail, I mention you in my morning and evening prayers. When I remember the tears you shed I really do get anxious to see you so I might be cheered up a bit. I have a vivid memory of the utterly sincere faith that's in you. I saw it first imbedded in your Grandma Lois and in your Mama Eunice and I am certain that it's in you too. So because I know you've got the stuff in you, I'm reminding you to shake the ashes off the God-given fire that's in you from the time I ordained you. For God has not given us the heart of a coward but of a strong man filled with love and self-discipline. So don't you ever be ashamed to stand up for our Lord, or for me, his prisoner. Rather, with God's help, get in the swim with others who are suffering for the gospel. For it is *God* who rescued us and invited us with a special invitation, not because we deserved it but because of his own inclination and kindness. Actually he extended the invitation through Christ Jesus before time began, but now he has made it clear and plain by the earthly appearance of our Life Guard, Christ Jesus. It was he who deactivated death and, through the great story, brought to light life and health. To establish this I was made a proclaimer, an agent and a teacher. That's the reason, too, that I get into all this trouble. But I'm not griping about it, because I'm not in the dark as to whom I've committed my life, and I'm quite confident that he is fully capable of taking care of my "deposit" under any condition.

13. Use the sermons you heard me preach as an example of sound preaching in Christian faith and love. Protect that wonderful "deposit" made by the Holy Spirit, whose house we are.

15. You know, don't you, that all those Texas folks let me down, including Findlay and Hardy. May the Lord bless the Butterfinger family, though, because he frequently invited me over and was not ashamed of my jail record. In fact, when he came to New Orleans he looked all over for me—and found me! May the Lord bless him with his mercy on the Big Day! And you know better than I about all the ways he helped me out in Birmingham.

2.

1. So then, my boy, as one who is a member of the Christian movement, be real spunky. And all that you heard from me through many sources you should place in the hands of committed men, who in turn will be capable of teaching others. As a good soldier of Christ Jesus take your share of the suffering. A man on active duty in the army gives up his private business in order to be free to carry out the orders of his commander. Also, if one enters a contest, he is not given a prize unless he competes according to the rules. And too, the farmer who *produces* the crop must have priority in *eating* from it. Think about what I'm telling you, for the Lord will help you to know what it's all about.

8. Keep your eyes on Jesus Christ as I preached him to you—one of us in the flesh but made alive when he died. This is why I'm arrested and jailed like a criminal, *but they haven't locked up God's word.* So I keep on putting up with everything for the sake

of the converts, in order that *they* might get hold of the salvation
which, along with spiritual discernment, is in Christ Jesus. This
poem is true:

> For if we've shared his death, we shall also share his life;
> If we bear our suffering, we shall share his reign.
> If we renege, he will reject us.
> If we turn loose the faith, then he holds on to it,
> Because he can't disown himself.

14. Keep these issues alive, urging people before God not to
split hairs, which gets nowhere and confuses those who have to
listen. Get the lead out of your britches and stand yourself up
before God as a seasoned veteran, a skilled worker, correctly slic-
ing the word of truth. And don't waste your time on theological
twaddle, for it will actually increase paganism, and such junk will
spread like blood poisoning. An example of this are some professors[1] who have overshot the truth by saying that "God is dead,"[2]
and they've got the faith of some folks in a tizzy. But just the same,
God's cornerstone is still in place, and it reads: "The Lord knows
his true ones," and "Let all who call themselves Christians withdraw from evil." Now in every house of importance there are arti-
cles not only of gold and silver but also of wood and clay, and some
are valuable and some are cheap. So then if someone keeps his
life clean of those things which cheapen him he will be a valuable
article, highly prized, useful to his Owner, ready for any good
purpose. So turn your back on loose kid stuff, and in company
with those who have in utter sincerity joined the Lord's movement, set your heart on fairness, faith, love and peace. And don't
get involved in idiotic, playpen arguments, since you know that
they generate fights. Now the Lord's man ought never to fight but
to be friendly toward everybody, to be disciplined, not easily riled
up, one who puts his point across to his opponents with genuine
humility, hoping that God might give his opponents a change of

---

[1]Paul goes so far as to name them, Henry and Fred.
[2]In the Greek the phrase is "that the resurrection has come and gone."

mind so as to understand the truth. And when they do understand, they'll wise up to the fact that the Devil has had them in the palm of his hand all along, and they'll bust out of his trap.

3.

1. Now get this clear: In the final showdown[3] some mighty rough times will come to pass, for people will love nobody but themselves and their money. They'll be big talkers, big shots, blabbermouths, shirking responsibility for their parents, with no inner grace, no commitment, no tenderness, no integrity. They'll be devils, wild and fierce, with no regard for the right, informers, unbalanced, inflated, loving a good time rather than loving God. They have all the outward trappings of religion, but will have nothing to do with its inner power. I say, SHUN THEM. For some of these creeps worm into families and play footsie with silly little women who are already piled sky-high with sins, who are aroused by all kinds of passions and who are always experimenting but never able to come to any understanding of the truth. These people fight the truth like Jerry and Jumbo fought Moses. Their minds are polluted and they would never pass the test on faith. But they won't make much headway, because their idiocy will become clear to everybody, just as in the case of the above-named gentlemen.

10. But you, you have carefully observed my teachings, my conduct, my motive, my loyalty, my ability to take it on the chin, my love, my endurance. You've seen the persecutions and sufferings which came my way in Albany, Opelika and Biloxi, as well as

[3]The final showdown is between Christianity and the world—"the final age of this world." (NEB) This "showdown" obviously comes, not at the end of time, but whenever and wherever the gospel confronts the demonic powers of the present age. The people whom Paul describes in the following verses are already on hand, and their true nature will become apparent when Christians have the guts and the strength to face them. That's why Paul wants Timothy to be aware of them now and to form no alliance with them (v. 5). Thus, the "last (extreme) days" are the days of conflict between the gospel and a man-centered society, regardless of where or when it comes.

other troubles I had to put up with. Yet from it all the Lord rescued me. Furthermore, *everybody* who tries to live a life dedicated to Jesus Christ will be hounded, whereas the crooks and the hucksters will climb still higher up the ladder, fooling others and being fooled.

14. Now as for you, son, take your stand on the things you've learned and have been assured of, recognizing that you've studied various subjects and that from infancy you have known the Holy Scriptures which can wise you up to the salvation that comes through the kind of faith that was in Christ Jesus. Every God-breathed writing is helpful for enlightenment, for guidance, for correction, for instruction in right living, so that God's man may be outfitted and fully equipped for performing any good task.

4.

1. Here before God and Christ Jesus, who stands ready to judge both living and dead on the basis of his own earthly life and his movement, I'm pressing it upon you: preach the word; stay on your toes when you're on duty and off; challenge, admonish, encourage, using both tact and reason. For the time will come when they won't put up with the genuine gospel. Delighting only in what they hear, they'll hire a whole staff of preachers who'll give it to them the way they want it. They'll turn their attention away from the truth and will settle for book reports. But you, son, always stay on the beam, be nonviolent, work as one who bears good news, carry out your job.

6. But I, I am in the process of being sacrificed for the cause, and it's just about time for me to check out. I have played the Great Game; I have finished the last inning; I have stuck by the team. Ahead, the Trophy of Right Living is being prepared for me, and the Lord, the fair Umpire, will award it to me on the big day. And he will give one, not only to me, but to everybody who has loved the Real Man.

9. Please do all you can to get here quickly, because Damon, still in love with the wordly life, let me down. He went to Thomasville; Chris went to Alabama and Titus to South Carolina. Luke alone is beside me. Stop by for Mark and bring him with you, for he is helpful to me on the job. I sent Tic to Birmingham. That overcoat I left in Nashville with Carl, bring it when you come. And the books too, especially those expensive ones.[4] Mr. Alexander, the welder, sure did me a lot of harm. The Lord will pay him back for what he has done. You too should keep your eye on him, because he violently opposed our testimony.

16. At my first hearing no one stood up for me but they all ran out on me. May it not be held against them. But the Lord stood with me and put heart in me, so that through me the message might be carried out and the whole public might hear. I was also spared from a "lion's-mouth" sentence. The Lord will spare me from every mean act and will lead me safely into his spiritual movement. May all credit be given him from one age to another. Let it be so.

19. Say hello to Prissy and Adrian and to the Butterfinger family. Hank stayed on in Atlanta. I left Troy sick in Meridian. Please try to get here before winter. Rube and Dan and Len and Claud and all the brothers send their regards. The Lord be with your spirit.

> Best wishes to all of you,
> *Paul*

---

[4] The Greek word means "highly finished skins."

Titus

1.

1. From Paul, God's slave, Jesus Christ's agent. My business is the faith of God's special people and their understanding of the truth, so that they may have a genuine devotion based on confidence in spiritual life. Before the age of time, the ever truthful God was pregnant with this life. And in his own good time, he brought it forth in the great story which, by orders of our Savior-God, was entrusted to me.

To Titus, a true son in a common faith.

Grace and peace from Father-God and from Christ Jesus, our Savior.

5. The reason I left you in Arkansas was that you might tie up the loose ends there and organize some key men in each city. Just as I instructed you, such a man should be above reproach, faithful to his wife, and have loyal children who don't have a reputation for delinquency and running wild. For as manager of God's house, it is absolutely essential that the supervisor himself be above reproach, not stuck on himself, or short-tempered, or a wino, or a bully, or a money-lover. Instead he should be friendly to strangers, on the side of the good, sensible, decent, devoted and disciplined. He must have a good grasp of the Christian faith so as to be able both to instruct others with sound teachings and to give the right answers to those on the other side of the fence. And believe you me, there are plenty of the latter, especially among the religious people. They are unbridled, smooth-talking windbags whose mouths must be stopped. They are converting whole households by holding "revivals" just to collect the "love offerings." One of them—in fact, one of their own evangelists—has said: "Some Arkansans are born liars, low-down brutes, lazy gluttons." This statement is correct. And because it is, let them have it straight from the shoulder, so that they might be spiritually healthy and not hold on to religious myths and to the traditions of a society that hides its face from the truth.

15. To the clean-hearted all things seem clean, but to the filthy and faithless, nothing looks clean, because both their minds and consciences are dirty. They pretend to know God, but their lives deny it. They are stinkers, disobedient and not fit for anything worthwhile.

2.

1. Now you, Titus, speak out on clear Christian issues. Help the adult men to stay on the wagon, to be dignified, wise and solid in the faith, in love and in steadfastness. Likewise, help the adult women to behave like saints and not devils, not to be addicted to drink but to be well-mannered, that they might train the young women to be husband-lovers, child-lovers and not flighty, to be sincere, to be good housekeepers, just plain good, and obedient to their own husbands, so as to cast no reflection on God's word.

6. In the same manner encourage the young men to be level-headed, and you yourself lead the way on all these matters as an example of proper behavior. Do not compromise on Christian principles. Be upright and let your talk be so sound that they can't throw it back in your teeth. The opponent will then feel sheepish when he finds he has no criticism to level at us.

9. Let the workers be cooperative with their bosses on all matters and try to please them without a lot of back talk. They should not kill time on the job, but should prove that they are completely loyal and good, in order that they might beautify the teachings of our Savior-God in every way.

11. For God's undeserved kindness has burst in upon us, bringing a new lease on life for all mankind. It is challenging us to turn our backs on junk religion and worldly cravings, and to live wisely and rightly and devoutly right here and now. Thus we constantly anticipate the marvelous hope and the bursting in of the wonder of the great God and our Savior, Christ Jesus. He gave himself for us, that he might cut us loose from every bad habit and purge us until we are clearly a Christian group bent on doing right. These are the things you're to talk about, to preach on and to insist on with all your authority. And don't take any sass from *anybody.*

3.

1. Don't let them forget that they are to accept the authority of governing officials and obey them, to be on call for every worthwhile task, and to smear no one. They are to be nonviolent and level-headed, and extending every courtesy to all men. For we too were once crazy, rebellious, hoodwinked, addicted to the whole works of sex and "fun," leading lives of wickedness and boredom, hating our own guts and hating each other. But then, when a sense of responsibility and human concern burst upon us from our Savior-God—not because we ourselves were so smart but because *he* was kind to us—he put us on the right track by completely making us over and giving us a new outlook. This came from the Holy Spirit which he so generously poured out on us through Jesus Christ, our Savior. This means that we have been set right by his undeserved favor and have become participants in a spiritual life that has purpose.

8. What I've told you is absolutely correct, and I want you to really put your foot down on these matters. Those who have rested their weight on God will then be encouraged to be responsible for good deeds. Such behavior is not only excellent but also beneficial to people. But silly slogans and reports and "isms" and theological fights, you should shun like the plague, for they are useless and senseless. After one or two attempts to straighten out a bigot, excuse him. Realize that such a fellow has been brainwashed and is sinning, he himself being his own evidence.

12. When I send either Art or Tic to you, hurry and come to me at New Orleans, for I've decided to stay there through the winter. Do all you can to help professors Smith and Oliver on their way, so that they do not lack anything. Let our people be trained to be responsible for proper actions in meeting urgent needs, lest they become uninvolved.

15. All here join me in sending greetings to you. Say hello to those who love us as Christian brothers.

                              Best wishes to you all,
                              Paul

The Letter to Philemon

1. From Paul, Christ Jesus' prisoner, and Brother Timothy.

To Philemon, our beloved co-worker, and Sister Abbey, and Archie, our fellow fighter, and the church gathered at your house.

We wish you grace and peace from our Father-God and our Lord Jesus Christ.

4. You have constantly been in my prayers as I thanked God for the news of your love for all the Christians and of the life you lead based on the Lordship of Jesus. May your common life together stimulate you to a deeper understanding of all the advantages of being a Christian.

7. I personally got a lot of joy and comfort from your love because, brother, you really did make the members perk up.

8. There's a matter about which I as a Christian have every right to make a demand of you, but because of our mutual love, I'll rather make it a request. Being no other than Paul, an old man and now a prisoner for the cause of Christ Jesus, I want to make a request of you about my boy, Obie, whom I converted while in jail. Before his conversion he wasn't worth a dime to you, but now he is very valuable to both you and me. And though it tears my heart out, I'm sending him back to you. I wanted so much to hold on to him myself, so he could pinch-hit for you in waiting on me while I'm in jail for the gospel. But I wouldn't do a thing like that without your permission, because you might feel obligated to respond favorably, rather than doing it gladly from your heart.

15. Perhaps the reason he left you for a while was that you might have him with you always, no longer as your slave—far more than that—as your beloved brother. He is especially dear to me, and I'm sure he'll be even more so to you, both as a person and as a brother in the Lord. If then you count me your partner, treat him as you would me. If he has hurt you in any way, or is in debt to you, transfer it to my account. I, Paul, hereby pledge with my own signature to pay it. (I won't mention the fact that *you* owe *me* your own self.) Yes sir, brother, I'd even like to make a little profit on you for the Lord! Give me a bit of Christian encouragement, will you?

21. I have written to you like this because I am sure of a favorable response from you. In fact, I believe you'll do even more than I'm asking. And by the way, get that guest room ready for me, because I'm hoping to be released soon and will be coming your way.

23. Pat, my cell-mate in Christ Jesus, sends his greetings, as do Mark, Rusty, Damon and Luke, my co-workers.

25. May the unmerited favor of the Lord Jesus Christ be upon the spirit of you all.

Sincerely,
Paul